J. K. LASSER'S

HOW TO READ A FINANCIAL STATEMENT

BY THE
J. K. LASSER INSTITUTE

Published by Simon and Schuster
New York

HOW TO READ A FINANCIAL STATEMENT

Published by Simon and Schuster, Inc.
Simon and Schuster Building
Rockefeller Center
1230 Avenue of the Americas
New York, New York 10020
SIMON AND SCHUSTER and colophon are registered
trademarks of Simon & Schuster, Inc.

Designed by Irving Perkins Associates
Manufactured in the United States of America
1 2 3 4 5 6 7 8 9 10
ISBN: 0-671-30914-5

CONTENTS

CONTENTS

CHAPTER 6
SAMPLE ANALYSIS OF AN ANNUAL REPORT

J.K. LASSER'S
HOW TO READ A FINANCIAL STATEMENT

You do not have to have an accounting background to understand a financial statement. The basic structure of a financial statement is clear-cut, practical, and obvious. If you were asked to give a financial statement of your personal wealth, you would not hesitate to state it as a total of *what you own* less *what you owe*. The financial statement of a business follows the same structure and, when expressed in accounting terms, *what you own* is called *assets* and *what you owe* is called *liabilities;* the difference between assets and liabilities is called the *equity* or *capital* of the business. Businesses list assets, liabilities, and equity in a financial statement called a Balance Sheet.

You also know that a list of your assets and liabilities does not tell the whole story about your financial status. Your ability to earn current and future income is also vital. If your earnings prospects are dim, your statement of financial worth is incomplete. To present a fuller view of your financial viability, you must also provide a statement of current income. The same is true with a business. You want to know not only the financial structure of a company and its assets and liabilities, but also its record of current earnings. A business presents information of its current earnings in a Statement of Income. Thus, the Balance Sheet and the Statement of Income are two major financial statements which you must have to evaluate a business.

Once you have a Balance Sheet and a Statement of Income and know how to analyze the figures entered on them, you have a basis on which to make projections and further analysis with the aid of supplementary statements such as the statement showing changes in financial position and retained earnings.

The purpose of this book is to help you read these statements and interpret them for business and investment decisions.

We would like to acknowledge the contribution of George Werner, CPA, in the preparation of this book.

Bernard Greisman, Editor

CHAPTER 1

HOW TO READ A BALANCE SHEET

THE BALANCE SHEET LISTS WHAT A COMPANY OWNS AND OWES

The term "Balance Sheet" is a widely used and accepted accounting term. Unfortunately, it does not give an effective idea or description of the information listed under its heading on a financial statement. The term merely reflects an accounting convention that says that the assets of a company should equal its liabilities and capital. This is the traditional way accountants have presented data of a financial statement: On the left side of a page, they list assets; on the right side, they list liabilities and capital. As an abstraction, the Balance Sheet equation may be justified as showing the relative contributions to assets by creditors (liabilities) and by the owners (stockholders).

Here is a Balance Sheet listing following the traditional accounting form:

Assets		Liabilities	
Current Assets	$_____	Current Liabilities	$_____
Marketable Securities	_____	Long-Term Liabilities	_____
Fixed Assets	_____		
Intangible Assets	_____		
		Stockholders' Equity	
		Capital Stock	$_____
		Retained Earnings	_____
Total	$_____	Total	$_____

This is how this pattern fleshes out with figures.

Assets		Liabilities	
Current Assets	$ 3,000,000	Accounts Payable	$ 1,000,000
Marketable Securities	500,000	Bonds	2,000,000
Fixed Assets	5,000,000	**Stockholders' Equity**	
Intangible Assets	1,500,000	Capital Stock	5,000,000
		Retained Earnings	2,000,000
	$10,000,000		$10,000,000

WHAT ARE CURRENT ASSETS?

These are assets which generally can be or will be turned into cash within one year. On a Balance Sheet, they are listed in the relative order of their liquidity. The following are current assets:

CASH. Cash, the most obvious form of current asset, may be held in various types of deposits or accounts, such as cash in hand, bank deposits, and certificates of deposit.

Details of cash deposits are not shown on a Balance Sheet because such a breakdown has no significance for Balance Sheet purposes. Although the way a company handles temporary cash investments is important, any current return on cash investments is not a major income element of an industrial or commercial firm.

ACCOUNTS RECEIVABLE. This is money due to the company for the sale of goods or services. Accounts receivables are adjusted for allowance for bad debts. The allowance recognizes potential losses on current receivables. The amount of the allowance is set by management, usually on the basis of past company or industry experience.

INVENTORY. In a manufacturing firm, inventory includes raw materials, partly finished assets and finished units. The Balance Sheet generally lists the total of these units as a single item. The details of the inventory may be explained in a separate schedule or footnote in the annual or interim report.

The method used to value inventory affects the dollar amount of the inventory listed on the Balance Sheet. In inflationary times, if LIFO is used, Balance Sheet values will generally be lower than similar inventory quantities, valued under FIFO. LIFO and FIFO are discussed in Chapter 2.

WHAT ARE MARKETABLE SECURITIES?

Companies invest in the stock of other companies in the same way as individual investors do. A company may invest in stocks and bonds which may be sold at any time. Marketable securities are considered temporary investments and part of current assets unless management has decided to hold the securities for a long period of time. Marketable securities are generally reported at cost unless the market value of the securities has declined below cost; if so, the securities are listed at the lower market value. Paper or unrealized profits are not reflected on the Balance Sheet. The names of these investments may be identified in footnote data. If the company holds a substantial interest in publicly held stock, compare the value listed in the Balance Sheet with its current market value. You may find that the market value substantially exceeds the amount listed on the Balance Sheet; later disposition of the stock could be a source of future income.

A company may also have permanent investments in affiliated or subsidiary companies. A consolidated balance sheet eliminates the securities held in subsidiary companies so that the assets and liabilities of the subsidiaries are listed as an integral part of the parent company.

WHAT ARE FIXED ASSETS?

Fixed assets are land, buildings, equipment, and office furnishings. The proportion of fixed assets to other assets is in direct relationship to the needs of a business to use fixed assets for the production of income. For example, the property investment of a manufacturing firm will be substantially greater than that of a bank.

Fixed assets are listed at cost of acquisition less accumulated depreciation. Replacement cost information is generally provided by footnotes to an annual report. Some authorities hold that replacement cost has little significance if there are no current plans for replacement.

Depreciation is discussed in Chapter 2.

WHAT ARE PREPAID EXPENSES AND DEFERRED CHARGES?

Prepaid expenses are amounts paid for future services. Fire insurance premiums and advance rentals are examples of prepaid expenses.

Deferred charges are amounts paid for services which have already been performed. However, accounting rules require that the expenses be amortized, that is, written off, over a period of time. The unamortized amount of the expense is considered an asset. Moving

17

expenses, bond discounts, and certain pension costs are examples of deferred charges.

Prepaid expenses and deferred charges are generally not significant in evaluating the assets of the company.

Prepaid income taxes are explained in Chapter 4.

WHAT ARE INTANGIBLE ASSETS?

Intangible assets are goodwill, copyrights, trademarks, and patents.

GOODWILL. Goodwill is stated on a Balance Sheet if the company has purchased goodwill in the purchase of a business. Goodwill in this case is that part of the purchase price of a business which exceeded the book value of the assets of the business. Accepted accounting practice is to amortize the goodwill over the period of its useful life up to 40 years.

PATENTS. The real value of a patent depends on how much earnings it produces. A Balance Sheet figure usually based on the cost of acquiring the patent does not reflect this value.

TRADEMARKS AND COPYRIGHTS. These intangibles are amortized over a period of time as determined by management. The method and estimated useful lives of these assets should be adequately disclosed in the financial statements.

WHAT ARE CURRENT LIABILITIES?

Current liabilities are debts incurred by the company in the ordinary course of business that are payable within one year or the normal operating cycle of the business if longer than one year. These are generally accounts payable owed to parties with whom the firm does business.

Accrued expenses are expenses that have been incurred but not yet paid, such as wages that have not been paid to employees because the end of the fiscal year of the company fell in the middle of a pay period. Similarly, accrued taxes are taxes which the company has not paid because the due date of payment occurs after the end of the company fiscal year.

Company liabilities may include loans from banks. Short-term borrowing is not a sign of weakness, especially if borrowing reflects seasonal loans that are paid after the close of the active sales period. Outside financing may be in order if interest paid is less than the rate that the company can earn by investing funds in its operations.

Short-term loans which exceed cash and receivables may be evidence that a company relies on bank loans for working capital.

A portion of originally long-term debt which is payable within a year is shown as a current liability.

Advances from customers or revenues received but not yet earned are listed as current liabilities if the obligation to perform services is to be met within one year.

WHAT IS LONG-TERM DEBT?

Long-term debt, as the term implies, is money borrowed by the company, payment of which is due more than a year after the end of the company fiscal year. The Balance Sheet will list the item without further explanation. However, the general nature and terms of long-term debt may be listed in a separate schedule of an annual report. Review the extent and terms of such debt to determine whether the company debt is reasonable in light of current economic conditions. When the debt is substantial, it is important to know when repayment of principal is required in order to weigh the ability of the company to meet the maturity requirements.

Where a company originally borrowed at interest rates below the current market rate, the company may be in a position to profit by buying back the bonds at a price below the face amount of the bonds.

WHAT IS STOCKHOLDERS' EQUITY?

The equity of the stockholders represents the money invested by the stockholders and retained profits not paid out as dividends.

A company may issue one class of stock or several classes, such as preferred and common. Common stock gives its owner the right to vote for directors and on certain corporate decisions and to share in corporate earnings when dividends are declared. Common stockholders have a liquidating share in a business after creditors and preferred stockholders are paid off.

Preferred stock is a cross between common stock and a bond. Preferred stockholders are guaranteed a fixed dividend annually and in a liquidation are paid off after creditors but before common stockholders. The amount of the dividend is fixed by the terms of the stock issue. The dividend rate may be a dollar amount, such as $5 per share, or a percentage of par value. Under the terms of the issue, preferred stock may be subject to call or redemption at a fixed price.

Stock may have a par value or no par value. Par value indicates the amount of capital paid in for each share by the original subscribers. The par value or the total dollar value of the capital stock does not have any relationship to market price. It represents the maximum liability (per share) to the stockholder in the event of the bankruptcy of the company.

WHAT ARE STOCK OPTIONS AND TREASURY STOCK?

A stock option represents a right to buy a certain number of shares of stock at a specified price within a certain period of time. Stock options are usually given to employees as part of a benefits or bonus program. The options have a specified life span and if not exercised, they are lost. When an executive exercises his option, the stock is purchased from the company's own Treasury Stock, not in the open marketplace. The difference between the exercise price and what the company originally paid for reacquiring its Treasury Stock is charged or credited to the Paid-In Capital account.

Treasury Stock is company stock that the company has reacquired through purchase or gift. It is not considered part of the outstanding stock. The cost of Treasury Stock is deducted on the Balance Sheet from the total of stockholder equity; *see* the sample annual report at the end of this book for a Balance Sheet showing this treatment.

STATEMENT OF RETAINED EARNINGS

A statement of retained earnings shows changes in retained earnings over several accounting periods. The statement is helpful in reviewing the ability of the company to pay dividends as it shows the growth or decline in earnings over the reporting periods.

STATEMENT OF RETAINED EARNINGS

	Year End Dec. 31	
	1984	1983
Retained Earnings at Beginning of Year	$190,000	$150,000
Plus Net Income for Year	100,000	75,000
	290,000	225,000
Less Dividends for Year	50,000	35,000
Retained Earnings at End of Year	$240,000	$190,000

THE NEXT STEP

You now have a working knowledge of the various items which are listed on a Balance Sheet. However, a cursory reading of labelled numbers will provide you no meaningful data. Looking at a Balance Sheet, you may be impressed by substantial cash assets which you feel indicate success. But you would be wrong if cash plus later collections of receivables were insufficient to meet the payables as they came due. Similarly, accounts receivable may have a golden glitter until a comparison with sales volume reveals that almost 50 per cent of the sales are still uncollected. Thus a business may have what seems to be a good current financial position, and yet be losing ground. You would not clearly see these conditions unless you knew how to analyze the figures.

The methods of analyzing are discussed in Chapters 4 and 5.

Finally be aware that the appearance of figures carried out to the dollar in a statement is in no way a guarantee of exactness. A dollar amount posted for cash means exactly what it says; that on the date of the Balance Sheet the company had cash of $5,000,000. However, a dollar amount given to inventory or to depreciation turns on valuations based on accounting conventions. Depreciation and inventory valuation methods give varying dollar amounts. Various elections are discussed in the following chapter.

CHAPTER 2

HOW TO READ A STATEMENT OF INCOME

IMPORTANCE OF STATEMENTS OF INCOME

The Statement of Income gives you the "bottom line"—the profit or loss of the company for a particular period. The Income Statement of current and past years will reveal the earning power of a company and provide a basis for projecting future earnings, also taking into consideration the state of the economy's technology and competition faced by the company.

Statements of Income are given in report form. The details within a Statement of Income vary according to the type of operations or services performed by the company. A retail or manufacturing company will provide details of cost of goods sold; a service corporation will not.

HOW TO READ A FINANCIAL STATEMENT

The following is the report pattern of a Statement of Income modeled after a retail operation:

MERCHANDISING CORPORATION
STATEMENT OF INCOME
FOR YEAR ENDED DECEMBER 31, 1984

Net Sales		$_____
Less:		
Cost of Goods Sold		_____
Gross Profit on Sales		_____
Less:		
Selling Expenses	_____	
General & Administrative		
Expenses	_____	
Total Expenses		_____
Income Before Income Taxes		_____
Less:		
Income Taxes		_____
Net Income for Year		$_____

A Statement of Income in an annual or interim report of a publicly held company will show amount of dividends paid out of net income as follows:

Weighted average common shares	
outstanding	_____
Earnings per share of common stock	$_____
Dividends per share of common stock	$_____

A Statement of Income in a report of a publicly held company will also show the income and expense items of prior years for comparison purposes. The following is an abbreviated form of Statement of Income showing the current and prior years.

STATEMENT OF INCOME

	Year ended September 30, 1983	1982
NET SALES	$313,719,923	$320,386,783
COSTS AND EXPENSES		
Cost of products sold	154,425,773	161,433,077
Advertising, promotion and selling	147,514,240	144,139,352
Total costs and expenses	301,940,013	305,572,429
Operating profit	11,779,910	14,814,354
OTHER EXPENSE		
Interest expense	6,640,912	6,375,807
Other, net	127,386	(632,993)
Total other expense (income)	6,768,298	5,742,814
Earnings before income taxes	5,011,612	9,071,540
PROVISION FOR INCOME TAXES	1,103,000	2,471,000
Net earnings	$ 3,908,612	$ 6,600,540
Net earnings per share	$1.01	$1.73

REVIEW OF SALES INCOME

You want to know if sales earnings are stable, increasing, or decreasing.

If the company sells several lines of merchandise, review a sales breakdown according to product lines.

Check the growth and stability of each line. A gross sales figure is meaningless unless the component lines are known. A gross amount may cloak a decline in

27

a major line and a nonrecurring increase in a minor product line.

The following is an excerpt of a breakdown of product lines explaining the Statement of Income of Food Corporation:

FOOD CORPORATION

	1984	1983
(DOLLARS IN MILLIONS)		
Net sales		
Consumer	$ 75.2	$ 88.4
Industrial	107.3	108.1
Agriculture	52.0	55.7
Away-From-Home Eating	9.1	7.5
Total Net Sales	$243.6	$259.7
Net Earnings		
Consumer	$ 2.1	$ 2.8
Industrial	4.2	3.7
Agriculture	2.0	1.5
Away-From-Home Eating	.4	.8
Total Net Earnings	$ 8.7	$ 8.8

You also want to determine if accounting methods have deflated or inflated earnings. Accounting elections for inventory, depreciation, and expense items affect the amount of income and loss reported.

Also consider the effect of inflation. An increase in income may be attributable to a rise in the general price level, not to decisions taken by management. Inflation will also have the effect of increasing expenses. Similarly, fluctuations in income may arise from events beyond the control of management, such as embargoes, strikes, and natural catastrophes.

Have net earnings moved in line with sales volume? If not, try to spot the reasons for the decline in earnings. Have they been caused by increased taxes or expenses or selling price reductions? Increased selling activity will tend to increase the cost of selling. Administrative expenses may also increase if an overall sales growth requires more people in the billing and accounts receivable department. An increase in sales volume which gives a low return may not justify an increase in expenses.

COST OF GOODS SOLD

An annual report may give the details of cost of goods sold in a separate schedule in the following type of breakdown:

Inventory, January 1	$ 20,000
Plus: Purchases	85,000
Goods Available for Sale	105,000
Less: Inventory December 31	25,000
Cost of Goods Sold	$ 80,000

The cost of goods sold of a manufacturing firm includes raw materials, wages and salaries of factory employees, utilities, depreciation on factory equipment and other factory overhead costs. These expenses are directly related to the manufacturing operations. Sell-

29

ing, general, and administrative expenses are not considered direct costs of production and are not included in cost of goods sold.

HOW INVENTORY VALUES AFFECT COST OF GOODS SOLD

The two basic ways of valuing inventory are "first-in, first-out" (FIFO) and "last-in, first-out" (LIFO). A business elects the method which meets its operating and financial objectives. In inflationary periods, LIFO tends (1) to reduce current earnings by increasing costs of goods sold and (2) to lower Balance Sheet inventory values; FIFO tends (1) to increase current earnings and (2) to increase the Balance Sheet inventory values (see example below).

Under FIFO it is assumed that the first goods purchased are used or sold first. Thus cost of goods sold is based on the cost of goods purchased earlier and the value of closing inventory is based on the cost of the most recently purchased units. Under LIFO, it is assumed that goods purchased last were sold or used first. Thus cost of goods sold is based on the cost of goods purchased toward the end of the year and closing inventory is valued on the basis of the cost of earlier purchases.

Example—

B Co.'s beginning inventory for the year was 20 units priced at $3 per unit. During the year, it made the following purchases:

Date	Quantity	Price per unit	Total sold
Jan. 5	5	$3.20	$ 16.00
May 6	10	4.00	40.00
Aug. 4	10	4.50	45.00
Dec. 20	20	3.50	70.00
	45		$171.00

Closing inventory at the end of the year showed 25 units.

Market value at that date is $3.50. This is how the inventory would be valued under:

First-in first-out (FIFO):

Inventory:

20 units @ $3.50	$ 70.00
5 units @ 4.50	22.50
25	$ 92.50

Cost of goods sold:

20 units @ $3.00	$ 60.00
5 units @ 3.20	16.00
10 units @ 4.00	40.00
5 units @ 4.50	22.50
40	$138.50

Last-in first-out (LIFO):

Inventory:

20 units @ $3.00	$ 60.00
5 units @ 3.20	16.00*
25	$ 76.00

Cost of goods sold:

20 units @ $3.50	$ 70.00
10 units @ 4.50	45.00
10 units @ 4.00	40.00
40	$155.00

* The excess of units over the beginning inventory was priced at the cost of the first year's purchases. They could also have been priced at the average cost of the year's purchases or at the cost of the last purchase. Other rules of computing LIFO have not been discussed here as they are within the scope of a professional accounting text.

DEPRECIATION

The fixed assets—machinery, buildings, autos, trucks, fixtures, and furniture—are used over a period of time to produce income. Therefore, accountants follow the practice of writing off the cost of a fixed asset over a useful life selected for the asset. The writeoff is called depreciation and is an expense deduction from income.

Useful life has usually no relation to actual use of the asset, especially since the tax laws have encouraged the use of accelerated depreciation rates and short useful lives which have no relation to the period a business actually uses the asset.

Shorter useful lives and the accelerated rates do not give any greater depreciation than the cost investment in an asset. But they give a business an opportunity to advance the time of taking deductions which in turn reduces income subject to taxes. This is a decided advantage where the immediate increased annual deductions will provide cash for working capital. That is, by taking increased deductions over a shorter period, the company defers the payment of taxes that would be due if it claimed smaller depreciation deductions, using more conservative methods of depreciation. The tax deferral lasts until the rapid method provides less depreciation deductions than the more conservative method would provide. The favorable tax position may be restored through purchases of new equipment.

HOW TO READ A STATEMENT OF INCOME

The following example illustrates how depreciation elections affect the reporting of income.

Example—

Company A and Company B are competitors, have the same amount of fixed assets, and report income of $200,000 before depreciation. Company A elects accelerated depreciation and claims depreciation of $50,000 resulting in a net income of $150,000. Company B, following a more conservative approach, takes straight line depreciation and claims depreciation of $35,000 resulting in a net income of $165,000. If only net income were compared, an observer would conclude that Company B is the more profitable company. However, a review of depreciation methods would show that there was no difference between the income-producing capacities of the two companies.

Once an investment is made in a depreciable asset, depreciation claimed over the useful life period does not involve any outlay of cash. For example, a company may show a loss which arises from substantial depreciation deductions and yet have cash with which to make distributions. That is because the loss stemming from the depreciation did not involve the payment of cash. The non-cash nature of depreciation is recognized in the Statement of Change in Financial Position, *see* chapter 4.

The depreciation charges are accumulated on the Balance Sheet in an account called accumulated depreciation, which is a direct offset to the fixed asset accounts. As the assets are periodically written off, the net value approaches zero, until subsequent purchases increase the values.

THE EFFECT OF THE INVESTMENT TAX CREDIT ON REPORTING INCOME

The way a company treats the investment tax credit affects income reporting. The credit, claimed on property purchased by the company, reduces the tax in the year the property is put into service. The credit provides substantial tax savings. For financial accounting purposes, a company may treat the credit in one of two ways:

1. It may follow the tax treatment and reduce reported tax expense in the year the equipment is put into service. This approach is called the *flow-through method*.
2. It may use the credit to reduce the cost basis of the property and thus spread the tax savings over the useful life of the asset. This is called the *deferral* or *amortization* method.

Actual tax payments are not affected by the accounting method used. The taxes are reduced by the amount of the credit in the year the property is put into service, and depreciation deductions for tax purposes are generally based on the actual cost of the property.

If a company elects the flow-through method, it will

show higher earnings in the year in which the credit is claimed because of a lower tax expense. A firm with comparable earnings and tax would show lower earnings if it used the deferral method for financial reporting. Further, in a year in which a company has made a substantial property acquisition, the tax credit under the flow-through method will affect the earnings of the company.

Accounting authorities prefer companies to use the deferral method. However, Congress has passed a law prohibiting any professional accounting body to require companies to use the deferral method.

FURTHER ANALYSIS OF THE STATEMENT OF INCOME

In the next chapter, you will learn how to apply percentages and ratios to the Statement of Income.

CHAPTER 3

HOW TO ANALYZE FINANCIAL STATEMENTS

MAKING SENSE OF THE FIGURES

Dollar amounts of financial statement items are mute testimony unless analyzed. Financial statements may be compared to meters on a highly complicated machine; each meter gives a numerical value. It is up to you to observe the figures, analyze them, and then decide if everything is operating correctly, and if not, what is wrong.

In the case of financial statements, analysis is based on comparing related items. You can visualize the importance of discovering relationships when you think of the proportions of human beings. A man with a 48-inch chest and a 40-inch waist is not in such bad shape. But a man with a 32-inch chest and a 40-inch waist had better watch his calories. Therefore, to answer the question what "shape" or condition a business is in, you have to be aware of structural relationships. For example, a $50,000,000 profit may be a good performance for one business, but not for another with very large capital investment. You make comparisons by developing percentages and ratios between related items.

PERCENTAGE CHANGES. Percentages are helpful in comparing data over two or more accounting periods. You select a base year and a comparison year. You compute the percentage of change by dividing the amount of the change between the two years by the base amount.

Example—

	Company A	
	1984	1983
Sales	$10,200,000	$10,000,000

	Company B	
	1984	1983
Sales	$ 700,000	$ 500,000

In both companies, sales increased by $200,000, but when percentages are calculated, you find that the increase in sales in Company A amounts to only 2% ($200,000 ÷ $10,000,000); in B, the increase was 40% ($200,000 ÷ $500,000).

RELATIVE PERCENTAGES. The relative position of items within statements are highlighted by converting the dollar values into percentages. For example, individual classes of assets may be expressed as a percentage of total assets and items in a Statement of Income may be expressed as a percentage of sales.

37

Example—

Net Sales	$100,000	100%
Cost of Goods Sold	60,000	60%
	40,000	40%
Expenses	30,000	30%
Net Income	$ 10,000	10%

RATIO. A ratio states the proportion or the relation of one amount to another. For example, relating $40,000 of current assets to $20,000 of current liabilities, we can say that their ratio is $40,000 to $20,000. Or, using mathematical notation, we can write it as $40,000 : $20,000, or, to put it more simply, 2 : 1. A ratio may also be expressed as a

$$\text{Fraction,} \quad \frac{2}{1}$$

Decimal, 2.0

Percentage, 200%

Rate, 2 times

Expressing relationships in ratios and percentages reduces larger numbers to simple terms which you can easily compare with other ratios of similar figures. You are probably familiar with the use of percentages to compare rates of return on investments.

Example—

You invest $157,000 in B company and get $11,000 in return. You invest $303,000 in the C company and get $14,000 in return. By dividing earnings by your initial investment, you find that your return from the B company is 7%; and from

C company, 4.6%. The percentages give you an efficient way of reducing two sets of figures to simple and common terms for easier comparison.

When you compare the figures of one period with those of another, be sure to compare figures for equivalent periods. For example, if you compare the first quarter of one year with the third quarter of the next year, you may very well be comparing the slow season in one year with the largest income-producing period of the next year. An apparent improvement would, in such a case, be meaningless.

When you compare a company with a competitor, you must make certain that they have similar operations and accounting methods. Different accounting methods will distort the reporting of earnings.

In the following pages, you will find tests for analyzing financial statements. Some were developed by creditors to determine whether a company is able to repay loans made to it; other tests were developed to guage the business efficiency of the company; still others measure how well the company earned income on its capital.

Here is a summary of the ratios discussed in this chapter.

Ratio	Formula	Use
• Return on total assets	$$\frac{\text{Net Income Before Interest Expense}}{\text{Average Assets}}$$	Measures how well the company earns money on capital supplied by creditors and stockholders
• Return on stockholders' equity	$$\frac{\text{Net Income Before Interest Expense}}{\text{Average Stockholder Equity}}$$	Measures how well company earns money on stockholder equity
• Return on your investment	$$\frac{\text{Annual Dividend Per Share}}{\text{Price Paid for Share}}$$	Measures return on your stock investment
• Price-to-earnings ratio	$$\frac{\text{Market Price Per Share}}{\text{Earnings Per Share}}$$	Measures price of stock in terms of earnings. The figure may be used to compare earnings with those of other firms.
• Book value of common stock	$$\frac{\text{Net Worth (Less Preferred)}}{\text{Common Shares Outstanding}}$$	Book value represents common stockholder's equity in company. Increases in book value over a period of one year may be evidence that the company is plowing back earnings.
• Equity to assets ratio	$$\frac{\text{Stockholder Equity}}{\text{Total Assets}}$$	Measures how much of company assets are financed by stockholders

Ratio	Formula	Description
• Earnings per share of common stock	$\dfrac{\text{Net Income (Less preferred dividend)}}{\text{Outstanding Common Shares}}$	Measures amount of net income available for dividends to common stockholder
• Debt ratio	$\dfrac{\text{Total Debt}}{\text{Total Assets}}$	Measures proportion of assets financed through debt
• Current ratio	$\dfrac{\text{Current Assets}}{\text{Current Liabilities}}$	Measures ability of company to pay current debts
• Acid ratio	$\dfrac{\text{Current Assets (Less Inventory)}}{\text{Current Liabilities}}$	Measures ability of company to pay debts without liquidating inventory
• Inventory turnover	$\dfrac{\text{Cost of Goods Sold}}{\text{Average Inventory}}$	Measures company efficiency in selling its products
• Operating ratios	$\dfrac{\text{Operating Expenses}}{\text{Net sales}}$	Helpful in comparing current company performance with those of prior years and of competing firms
• Accounts receivable turnover	$\dfrac{\text{Net Sales}}{\text{Average Accounts Receivable}}$	Measures company efficiency in collecting accounts receivable

RETURN ON TOTAL ASSETS
OR INVESTMENTS

Here you measure company success in earning money on its capital. There are two approaches, depending on the way you treat capital. You can treat capital as all funds contributed by creditors and owners or as capital contributed by the stockholders.

The percentage return on total capital measures how much a company earns on all its capital, rather than just the equity interest. You start with net income and add back interest paid to bondholders. Net income is then divided by average total assets. The average total assets is figured by adding together the total assets at the beginning and the end of the year and dividing by two.

$$\frac{\text{Net Income Before Interest Expense}}{\text{Average Assets}}$$

Example—

Net Income	$ 75,000
Add Back Interest Paid to Bondholders	15,000
Net Income Before Interest Income	$ 90,000
Total Assets at Beginning of Year	800,000
Return on Total Assets $\dfrac{\$90,000}{\$900,000}$	10%

If you restrict the ratio to stockholder equity, you divide net income by average stockholder interest. The average stockholder interest is figured by adding together the equity interest at the beginning and the end of the year and dividing by 2.

Example—

Net Income Before Interest Expense	$ 90,000
Equity at Beginning of Year	750,000
Equity at End of Year	850,000
Average Equity	$800,000

Return on stockholder equity is $\dfrac{\$90,000}{\$800,000}$ 11.3%

RETURN ON YOUR INVESTMENT

If you have invested in stock for a return of income, you want to know what percentage of income you are making on your investment. You may do this by dividing the annual dividends paid per share by the price you paid for each share.

$$\frac{\text{Annual Dividend Per Share}}{\text{Price Paid for Share}}$$

Example—

You paid $10 per share and receive a dividend of 80 cents per share. Your return on your investment is 8% $\left(\dfrac{\$.80}{\$10}\right)$.

If the return is below the rate paid by other available investments, you should consider a switch of investment unless you are holding the stock for a capital gain on later sale.

43

PRICE-TO-EARNINGS RATIO

The price-to-earnings ratio allows you to compare the income earnings of a company with the earnings of competing firms. The ratio also helps you determine whether the market price of the stock is commensurate with its earnings. You figure the ratio by dividing the current market price of the stock by earnings reported per share.

$$\frac{\text{Market Price Per Share}}{\text{Earnings Per Share}}$$

Example—

The market price of a share of stock is $30; its earnings per share is $3 a share. The price-to-earnings ratio is 10 $\left(\frac{\$30}{\$3}\right)$. The stock is selling for 10 times the earnings per share.

BOOK VALUE PER SHARE
OF COMMON STOCK

You find the book value per share of common stock by dividing net worth (less value of preferred stock if any) by common shares outstanding.

$$\frac{\text{Net Worth (Less Preferred)}}{\text{Common Shares Outstanding}}$$

Example—

Common Stock	$ 720,000
Retained Earnings	380,000
Net Worth	$1,100,000
Common Shares Outstanding	100,000
Book Value Per Share ($1,100,000 ÷ 100,000)	$11

Book value as an analytical standard is limited. It presents no measure of the liquidation value of industrial companies because on forced sales, assets are generally sold at prices below the value listed on the Balance Sheet. On the other hand, book value may be significant in determining the value of stock investments in banks, investment companies, and insurance companies which own substantial liquid assets.

Despite the limitations of book value, some investors use book value to check whether the market price of a stock is reasonable. Book value may also have some utility where there is a possibility that the company may be involved in a merger in which book value would be considered in fixing the terms of an exchange of stock.

EQUITY-TO-ASSET RATIO

The equity ratio tells you how much of the total assets are financed by the stockholders. You compute it by dividing total stockholders' equity by total assets.

$$\frac{\text{Stockholders' Equity}}{\text{Total Assets}}$$

Example—

Total Assets	$1,200,000
Total Stockholders' Equity	$ 700,000
Equity Ratio $\dfrac{\$\ 700,000}{\$1,200,000}$	58%

Where substantial capital is provided by creditors, a company will show a low equity ratio. A low equity ratio is favorable to the shareholders as long as the rate earned on total assets exceeds the rate of interest paid to creditors; however, where substantial debt is carried there is the possibility that a decline in income may prevent the company from meeting interest and principal and force a liquidation or reorganization of the business. If a company shows a low equity ratio you should check the capacity of the business to produce a return exceeding the cost of debt obligation and the stability of the earnings.

EARNINGS PER SHARE OF COMMON STOCK

As a common stockholder, you want to know the amount of net income available as dividends to the common stockholders. Earnings per share are listed generally below the Statement of Income. If not, you figure earnings per share as follows: (1) You reduce net income by preferred dividend requirements, and (2) divide adjusted net income by the number of shares of common stock outstanding.

$$\frac{\text{Net Income (Less Preferred Dividends)}}{\text{Outstanding Common Shares}}$$

Example—

Net Income	$100,000
Less Preferred Dividends	10,000
Net Income Available for Common Stock	90,000
Shares of Stock Outstanding	15,000
Earnings Per Share $\dfrac{\$90,000}{15,000}$	$6.00

If a company has convertible bonds or preferred stocks, warrants, or options outstanding which may affect per-share earnings by more than three percent, the company lists primary earnings per share and fully diluted earnings per share. The primary earnings per share figure is arrived at by dividing net income after preferred dividends by common shares outstanding plus dilutive common share equivalents with securities whose dividend or coupon rate at the time of issue is less than two-thirds the prime rate at that time. Options and warrants are regarded as common stock equivalents at all times. The fully diluted earnings per share figure assumes that all outstanding securities would be converted and that would reduce earnings per share.

Earnings per share allows you to compare the performance of the company over a period of years.

DEBT RATIO

The debt ratio is found by dividing total debt by total assets. It gives the proportion of assets financed through borrowing.

$$\frac{\text{Total Debt}}{\text{Total Assets}}$$

Example—

Total Debt		$300,000
Total Assets		900,000
Debt Ratio $\dfrac{\$300,000}{\$900,000}$		33⅓%

The reasonable amount of debt depends on the type of business and the stability of its income. A public utility may carry a substantial debt safely because of its earnings and stability, whereas the same proportion of debt in an industrial firm may be unacceptable if its earnings are subject to shifting market forces.

Creditors prefer a lower debt ratio as it indicates that there is a margin of safety in case of a loss of value in assets.

TEST FOR BONDHOLDERS

The safety of bond investments is checked by determining the number of times interest is earned.

NUMBER OF TIMES INTEREST IS EARNED. This tests the extent to which net income covers interest payment requirements.

$$\frac{\text{Operating Income Before Income Taxes and Interest}}{\text{Annual Interest Expense}}$$

Example—

Operating Income (before deductions for interest and income taxes)	$100,000
Annual Interest Expense	$ 25,000
Times Interest Earned $\left(\dfrac{\$100,000}{\$25,000}\right)$	4

Earnings several times greater than the interest obligation shows that there is sufficient income to meet interest payments and other needs of the business.

CURRENT AND ACID RATIOS TEST ABILITY TO MEET CURRENT DEBTS

The Current Ratio gives you a measure of the ability of the company to pay its current obligations. You find the current ratio by dividing current assets by current liabilities.

$$\frac{\text{Current Assets}}{\text{Current Liabilities}}$$

Example—

Current assets are $600,000 and current liabilities are $100,000. The current ratio is 6 to 1 or 6 ($600,000/$100,000).

An industrial company is expected to have at least twice the amount of current assets as current liabilities or a ratio of 2 to 1; a utility may safely have a current ratio of 1 to 1 because of the nature of its monthly cash income flow.

Where a company is concerned about its credit rating, it may take "window-dressing" steps to improve its current ratio before the financial statement is prepared. It may do this by postponing purchases and paying its current liabilities. Also a current ratio computed for the end of a fiscal year may not reflect the usual current ratio if the fiscal year ends at the end of the business season. At that time, the current ratio may be higher.

Creditors prefer to see larger current ratios, although a high current ratio may be a sign that assets are not being used effectively to produce income.

ACID TEST. A company may have an acceptable current ratio; however, if a substantial amount of its current assets are in inventory, it could have liquidity problems if the inventory could not be sold quickly. You can test the company's "bare bones" liquidity by omitting inventory from current assets in figuring the ratio. This is the "acid test," which is the ratio of "quick" assets to current liabilities.

Quick assets are cash, marketable securities, and net accounts receivable (less the reserve for bad debts). The "acid test" gives a measure of the solvency of the business if operations stopped because the value of quick assets does not depend on the company continuing in business. Inventories and prepaid expenses are not considered in the acid test.

Expressed as a fraction, the acid ratio is:

$$\frac{\text{Cash and Marketable Securities} + \text{Net Accounts Receivable}}{\text{Current Liabilities}}$$

Generally, if the acid ratio is 1:1, or 100%, the business is considered to have passed the acid test. That is, the quick assets will cover the payment of all current liabilities. However, this ratio may not be an adequate test if the average time required to collect receivables is greater than the time extended by creditors for the payment of short-term liabilities.

TURNOVER OF INVENTORY

The purpose of figuring inventory turnover is to determine how fast a company sells its products. A high turnover ratio may indicate a strong demand for its products; a low one may mean it is facing strong competition or a decline in consumer interest.

$$\frac{\text{Cost of Goods Sold}}{\text{Average Inventory}}$$

Example—

The beginning inventory was $900,000; final inventory on December 31 is $700,000 and cost of goods sold is $6,000,000. The average inventory is $800,000 ($1,600,000 ÷ 2). The turnover ratio is 750% ($6,000,000 divided by $800,000). This means that the inventory turns over 7½ times during the year.

The ratio is not significant unless compared to ratios of prior years and those of comparable industries. Businesses, such as supermarket chains, which have a low profit margin will show a high turnover; businesses selling heavy equipment and machinery may traditionally show low turnovers. Also, compare inventory turnover with the gross profit rate. A high inventory turnover and a low gross profit reveal that a higher volume of business is necessary to produce a return for the company.

You figure the turnover ratio by dividing cost of goods sold by the average of year-end inventory and beginning inventory.

OPERATING RATIOS

You use operating ratios to compare current company performance with its performance in prior years and also with operating ratios of firms in the same industry.

You may compare the sum of cost of goods sold and operating expenses with net sales:

$$\frac{\text{Cost of Goods Sold} + \text{Operating Expenses}}{\text{Net Sales}}$$

Example—

Net sales are $100,000; cost of goods sold is $50,000, and operating expenses are $40,000. The operating ratio is 90%.

52

$$\frac{\$50,000 + \$40,000}{\$100,000} = 90\%$$

Thus the net operating income is 10% of sales (100% — 90%).

You may use an operating expense ratio to review the trend of operating expenses. You find the ratio by dividing operating expenses by net sales.

$$\frac{\text{Operating Expenses}}{\text{Net Sales}}$$

Example—

In 1984, operating expenses are $500,000, net sales, $1,500,-000. In 1983, operating expenses were $250,000 and net sales $1,000,000. The 1984 operating expense ratio is 30% ($500,-000 ÷ $1,500,000). In 1983, the operating expense ratio was 25% ($250,000 ÷ $1,000,000).

CHECKING THE ALLOWANCE FOR BAD DEBTS

The amount of bad debt allowances is fixed by management. As an outsider, you have no access to accurate data to determine whether the allowance is reasonable. But you can make observations by figuring the percentage of the allowance to receivables and comparing it with percentages in the same industry. A percentage lower than the norm may be evidence that the company has underestimated bad debts.

Example—

In 1983, accounts receivable were $45,620,000; bad debt allowances were $1,720,000; in 1982, accounts receivable were $51,149,000, the allowance, $900,000.

> The 1983 ratio: ($1,720 ÷ $45,620) is 3.7
> The 1982 ratio: ($900 ÷ $51,149) is 1.8

The increase in the bad debt allowance in one year was caused by poor business conditions which also caused a drop in receivables.

ACCOUNTS RECEIVABLE TURNOVER

The turnover of accounts receivable is figured by dividing net sales by the average of accounts receivable. The greater the number of times that accounts receivable turn over, the smaller is the amount of funds tied up in uncollected accounts.

$$\frac{\text{Net Sales}}{\text{Average Accounts Receivable}}$$

Example—

Net Sales	$477,017,000
Accounts Receivable at Beginning of Year	50,249,000
Accounts Receivable at End of Year	43,980,000
Average Accounts Receivable	$47,074,500
Accounts Receivable Turnover	

$$\frac{\$477,017,000}{\$\ 47,074,500} \text{ or 10 times during the year}$$

You can find the number of average days to turn over receivables by dividing 365 days by the receivable turnover figured in the above example.

Example—

In the above example the turnover rate was 10 times. This tells you that the average days needed to turn over receivables was about 37 days (365 ÷ 10).

Analysis of the average day's turnover depends on company credit terms and sales activity. If the company gives credit of up to 30 days, then collections at a 37-day rate may be adequate. According to Dun & Bradstreet, the collection period should not exceed the maturity period by more than 10 to 15 days. An increase in sales at the end of the year can distort the average as the receivables may include sales that will be paid in due course soon after the end of the year.

The proportion of receivables to annual sales should also be reviewed. An increase in receivables exceeding the normal sales pattern may indicate that the company has instituted a liberal credit policy to keep up the volume of sales.

SOURCES OF RATIOS AND OTHER FINANCIAL INFORMATION FOR ANALYSIS

Ratios and percentages are important only when they are compared with similar rates or percentages. Several publishers provide extracts of statements that are excellent research aids to review the position of a company within the economy and industry. They list many of the analytical ratios explained in this chapter.

Robert Morris Associates, a banking service organization, publishes *Annual Statement Studies* which lists assets, liabilities, and stockholders' equity, a percentage of total assets; income statement amounts expressed as a percentage of net sales; and key ratios (expressed as the median, the upper quartile, and the lower quartile for each industry). Data within each of the 223 industry groups are organized according to the size of the firm.

Dun & Bradstreet, Inc. annually publishes *Key Business Ratios* in 125 lines of business that are divided into retailing, wholesaling, manufacturing, and construction. A total of 14 ratios are presented for each of the 125 industry groups. They are: (1) current assets to current debt; (2) net profits on net sales; (3) net profits on tangible net worth; (4) net profits on net working capital; (5) net sales to tangible net worth; (6) net sales to net working capital; (7) collection period; (8) net sales to inventory; (9) fixed assets to tangible net worth; (10) current debt to tangible net worth; (11) total debt to tangible net worth; (12) inventory to net working capital; (13) current debt to inventory; (14) funded debts to net working capital.

You may also get useful information from the condensed data provided by Moody's Manual, Standard & Poor's Corporation, and Fitch Investor's Service.

GOVERNMENT SOURCES. The following agencies also provide data for different types of businesses: The Interstate Commerce Commission, the Federal Trade Commission, the Federal Power Commission, the Federal Communications Commission, the Securities and Exchange Commission, the Board of Governors of the Federal Reserve System, and the Board of Directors of the Federal Deposit Insurance Corporation.

CHAPTER 4

HOW TO READ STATEMENTS SHOWING CHANGES IN WORKING CAPITAL AND CASH FLOW

In the prior chapters, we have discussed many types of assets and liabilities and paid scant attention to cash. In this chapter, cash will be given its due. Cash is what the business game is all about. You invest cash in order to get at some point in time a greater amount of cash on the cash that you have invested, and the company in which you invest must earn cash to pay its bills and to pay dividends to you and others in the business. If, after all of its efforts, a company lacks cash to meet its obligations, it will fail.

The Balance Sheet and Statements of Income do not tell you all the sources of company cash and where it has been used. In fact, a company may show earnings on its Statement of Income and yet suffer a decline in cash. You have a means of reviewing the cash deployment of a company through the Statement of Changes in Financial Position, which provides this information in terms of working capital. Working capital is a good measure of cash resources because working capital is made up of cash and other liquid assets which can be converted into cash in a short period of time to meet the payment of short-term liabilities. Further, the Statement of Changes in Financial Position shows sources of cash transactions which do not appear in the Statement of Income, such as:

> The use of cash to pay off long-term debt.
> The use of cash to buy equipment for expanding plant facilities.
> The receipt of cash through the issuance of new stock.
> The receipt of cash through the issuance of long-term bonds.

WHAT IS WORKING CAPITAL?

Working capital, the difference between current assets and current liabilities, is the amount of current assets a company would retain if forced to pay all of its current liabilities.

Working capital tells you of the ability of the company to operate its normal business without financial restrictions, to expand without the need of new financing, and to meet emergencies. As working capital is a measure of a going concern, fixed assets are not included in working capital because they would not be sold to raise cash for current needs. A forced sale of fixed assets would signal a business failure.

An acceptable amount of working capital for a company varies with sales volume and the type of business the company transacts. Companies that are required to hold inventories for long periods of time need larger amounts of working capital in relation to sales.

Working capital increases when a company produces more working capital than is used in the business; working capital decreases when the business used more working capital than was produced during the year.

SOURCES OF WORKING CAPITAL

The sources of working capital are shown in a Statement of Changes in Financial Position. Among accountants, the statement is also called a Statement of Source and Application of Funds. The statement, as its name implies, shows the sources of working capital and uses of working capital.

The statement breaks down operational and nonoperational sources and uses of funds. There are items that have been deducted in arriving at net income that are added back since they do not require actual cash outlays. These are depreciation, amortization, deferred income taxes, and losses from the sale of assets. Dividends, capital expenditures, and debt repayments reduce working capital.

HOW TO READ STATEMENTS SHOWING CHANGES

The following is the general accounting outline of
the Statement of Changes in Financial Position and
Changes in Components of Working Capital. The statement lists the major sources of working capital, starting
with net income from operations and transactions that
use working capital, such as acquisitions of new equipment and the payment of dividends. The Changes in
Components of Working Capital give a breakdown by
category for each line in the Balance Sheet, but does not
give actual sources and uses of cash.

STATEMENT OF CHANGES IN FINANCIAL POSITION
Years Ended December 31, 19___, and 19___

	19___	19___
SOURCES OF WORKING CAPITAL		
Net Income	$_____	$_____
Add expenses not requiring the outlay of working capital:		
Depreciation and amortization		
Deferred income taxes		
Loss from sale of assets		
Working capital provided by operations		
From nonoperating sources		
Proceeds from issuing additional shares of stock		
Proceeds from sale of noncurrent assets (property and equipment)		
Proceeds from long-term financing		
Total sources		
USES OF WORKING CAPITAL		
Net loss		
Less expenses not requiring outlay of working capital		
Depreciation and amortization		

Retirement of long-term debt
Acquisition of noncurrent assets
(property and equipment)
Dividends paid
Repurchase of outstanding shares of
capital stock
Total uses

INCREASE (DECREASE) IN WORKING CAPITAL $ $

THE CHANGES IN COMPONENTS OF
WORKING CAPITAL

	19__	19__
INCREASE (DECREASE) IN CURRENT ASSETS		
Cash and marketable securities	$	$
Receivables		
Inventories		
Refundable Federal income taxes		
Prepayments		
INCREASE (DECREASE) IN CURRENT LIABILITIES		
Notes payable		
Current portion of long-term debt		
Accounts payable		
Federal and State income taxes		
Accrued expenses		
INCREASE (DECREASE) IN WORKING CAPITAL	$	$

The following statements are examples of a Statement of Changes in Financial Position extracted from an actual operating company, with an excerpt of a Balance Sheet showing current assets and current liabilities. The difference between the current assets and the current liabilities listed on the Balance Sheet is working capital. Here, working capital for 1984 was $137,525; for 1983, it was $129,039. The increase in working capital of $8,486 is explained in the Statement of Changes in Financial Position.

BALANCE SHEET (EXCERPT)
(In thousands)

	1984	1983
CURRENT ASSETS		
Cash	$ 31,135	$ 4,809
Accounts receivable	120,803	135,456
Inventories	48,592	69,077
Other current assets	1,292	1,405
Total current assets	$201,822	$210,747
CURRENT LIABILITIES		
Notes payable to banks, unsecured	$ —	$ 13,000
Accounts payable	34,790	42,299
Accrued interest	1,600	1,591
Dividends payable	1,948	1,940
Long-term debt due within one year	15,579	13,452
Other accrued liabilities	10,380	9,426
Total current liabilities	$ 64,297	$ 81,708
WORKING CAPITAL	$137,525	$129,039

STATEMENT OF CHANGES IN FINANCIAL POSITION
(In thousands)

	1984	1983
SOURCES OF WORKING CAPITAL		
Net income	$16,501	$39,045
Charges (credits) against income not involving working capital		
Depreciation	10,863	10,741
Deferred income	5,124	13,022
Deferred federal income tax	(9,067)	(12,767)
Other	(898)	(82)
Total from operations	22,523	49,959

Retirement of equipment	1,369	5,491
Increase in long-term debt	11,195	11,124
Other	1,689	284
Total from all sources	$36,776	$66,858

USE OF WORKING CAPITAL		
Additions to equipment	$ 5,596	$21,882
Cash dividends	7,771	7,803
Reduction of long-term debt	14,923	12,864
Other	—	3,908
Total uses	$28,290	$46,457
INCREASE IN WORKING CAPITAL	$ 8,486	$20,401

CHANGES IN COMPONENTS OF WORKING CAPITAL
(In thousands)

	1984	1983
INCREASE (DECREASE) IN		
CURRENT ASSETS		
Cash and short-term investments	$26,326	$(27,861)
Accounts receivable	(14,653)	57,187
Inventories	(20,485)	(56,052)
Other current assets	(113)	(67)
	$(8,925)	$(26,793)
INCREASE (DECREASE) IN		
CURRENT LIABILITIES		
Notes payable to banks, unsecured	$(13,000)	$13,000
Accounts payable	(7,509)	(41,954)
Accrued interest	9	(938)
Federal income tax	—	(10,903)
Dividends payable	8	390
Long-term debt due within one year	2,127	(1,304)
Other accrued liabilities	954	(5,485)
	$(17,411)	$(47,194)
INCREASE IN WORKING CAPITAL	$8,486	$20,401

Although operating revenues substantially declined, the company showed an increase in working capital as it had reduced the amount of its current liabilities at a rate exceeding the decrease in current assets. It had also acquired funds by increasing its long-term debt, and it used less funds to purchase equipment.

STATEMENT OF CHANGES ON A CASH FLOW BASIS

Instead of showing a Statement of Changes in Financial Position on a working capital basis, a company may prepare the statement in terms of explaining increases or decreases in cash alone. The statement based on cash flow is similar to a Statement of Working Capital. The advantage of a cash statement is that it highlights the flow of cash during the reporting period. However, for purposes of projecting the company's liquidity, a statement based on working capital is preferable because working capital includes liquid noncash items which can or will be turned into cash within a short period of time.

Examples of a Statement of Changes in Financial Position based on cash flow, extracted from an actual company, is on the next page. The increase in cash of $10,953,000 is explained in the statement.

BALANCE SHEET
(In thousands)

	1984	1983
ASSETS		
Current assets		
Cash	$ 15,866	$ 4,913
Accounts receivable	44,228	43,904
Inventories	41,111	44,503
Prepaid expenses	272	3,244
Total current assets	101,477	96,564
Fixed assets	17,168	15,430
Other assets	1,712	3,010
Total assets	$120,357	$115,004
LIABILITIES		
Current liabilities		
Notes payable	$ 300	$ 300
Accounts payable	43,123	42,353
Accrued income taxes	2,871	2,994
Accrued liabilities	3,536	3,262
Total current liabilities	49,830	48,909
Long-term debt	2,984	3,420
Total liabilities	52,814	52,329
SHAREHOLDERS' EQUITY		
Common stock	4,530	4,524
Paid-in capital	9,142	9,103
Retained earnings	53,871	49,048
Total shareholders' equity	67,543	62,675
Total liabilities, shareholders' equity	$120,357	$115,004

HOW TO READ STATEMENTS SHOWING CHANGES

STATEMENT OF CHANGES IN FINANCIAL POSITION

	1984	*1983*
Cash, beginning of year	$ 4,913	$ 1,496
FUNDS PROVIDED (USED) BY OPERATIONS:		
Net income	9,434	8,701
Items in net income not requiring the use of funds		
Depreciation and amortization	4,361	3,621
Deferred income taxes	4,026	(170)
Loss (gain) on sale of capital assets	17	(62)
Subtotal	17,838	12,090
Changes in working capital that provided (used) funds		
Accounts receivable	(324)	(5,139)
Inventory	3,392	1,994
Prepaid expenses	31	153
Refundable income taxes	—	453
Accounts payable	770	2,789
Income taxes currently payable	(1,344)	2,610
Accrued liabilities	274	(123)
Funds provided by operations	20,637	14,827
FUNDS PROVIDED BY (PAID TO) OUTSIDE SOURCES:		
Issuance of notes payable	—	1,500
Payment of notes payable	(300)	(150)
Cash dividends	(4,430)	(4,434)
Funds paid to outside sources	(4,730)	(3,084)
OTHER SOURCES (USES) OF FUNDS		
Net additions to property and equipment	(6,952)	(6,789)
Proceeds from sale of capital assets	743	72
Other assets	1,255	(1,609)
Other uses of funds	(4,954)	(8,326)
NET INCREASE (DECREASE) IN FUNDS	10,953	3,417
Cash, end of year	$15,866	$ 4,913

The increase in working capital was $3,992,000.

Current Assets—1984	$101,477	
Current Liabilities—1984	49,830	
1984 Working Capital		$51,647
Current Assets—1983	96,564	
Current Liabilities—1983	48,909	
1983 Working Capital		47,655
Increase in Working Capital		3,992

The disparity between the increase in working capital and the increase in cash stems from differences between accruals reflected in the computation of working capital and the cash transactions reflected in the cash flow statement.

Note: Some financial analysts have referred to cash flow as net income (after income taxes) plus depreciation. This shorthand approach is misleading because it ignores all other cash additions and uses. In the above example, this type of calculation would give a "cash flow" of $13,795,000, whereas the cash increase as shown by the statement is $10,953,000.

DEFERRED AND PREPAID INCOME TAXES

Differences between tax accounting rules and regular accounting rules may cause differences in reporting income or loss. The differences generally arise when for tax purposes income is deferred to a later year or deductions are accelerated in an earlier year.

HOW TO READ STATEMENTS SHOWING CHANGES

Example—

1. For income tax purposes, a company chooses to defer the reporting of sales income by electing the installment basis, but for financial purposes, it reports income in the year of sale under the regular accrual basis. As a result, lower income taxes are incurred than would have been payable under the accrual basis which the company uses for financial purposes.

2. For income tax purposes, accelerated depreciation bunches deductions in the earlier part of the useful life of an asset. Straight line depreciation spreads the deductions evenly over the useful life period. If a company elects accelerated depreciation for tax purposes but uses straight line for financial purposes, lower income taxes are reported for the earlier years than would have been payable if straight line had been used.

3. A company is engaged in long-term contract work. For tax purposes, it reports income when the contract is completed; for financial purposes, it reports income on the contract on the percentage of completion method.

In these cases, following accounting practice rules, a company computes for purposes of its financial statement the tax that would have been due if it had not made the favorable tax election. If the tax computed is larger than the actual tax liability, the difference between this income tax and the actual current income tax is called the deferred income tax. The sum of the deferred tax and the actual tax is a charge against current income on the Statement of Income and is usually identified as "provision for income taxes."

An annual report will generally break down the major components of items causing deferred tax.

Example—

In 1983, as a result of claiming accelerated depreciation, the income tax of a company is $50,000. If accelerated depreciation had not been claimed, the tax would have been $55,000. On the company report, this may be stated as follows:

Provision for income taxes

Current	$50,000
Deferred	5,000
	$55,000

In a footnote explaining the income tax, the item causing the deferred provision for income tax is explained. In this case, the explanation would be "excess of tax depreciation over financial statement depreciation."

On the Statement of Changes in Financial Position, the deferred tax is also shown as an adjustment which increases working capital because no cash was used to meet the expense. If the deferred tax is payable within the year, it is a current liability. If payable in a longer period it is a long-term liability.

Prepaid taxes. Differences in tax financial accounting rules may result in prepaid taxes. This may happen if taxable income exceeds accounting income; the difference between the two tax computations is treated as a prepaid tax and is reported as a prepaid asset on the Balance Sheet.

Example—

Under its accounting method, a car manufacturer for financial purposes charges the car warranties in the year in which the autos are sold. For tax purposes, however, the warranty charges are not deductible until they are incurred. In such a situation, more taxes are paid than are chargeable under accounting rules. The difference is the prepaid tax. The tax computed under the financial accounting method is $50,000,000. The actual current tax is $51,000,000. The difference of $1,000,000 is attributed to the fact that the cost of the warranties were not deductible in the year of sale, although for the financial purposes the deduction was claimed. The difference is called a prepaid tax.

CHAPTER 5

HOW TO READ AN ANNUAL REPORT

Each stockholder in a publicly held company must receive an annual report. Most companies not only send annual reports but also interim reports, usually on a quarterly basis. The interim report generally presents the Income and Balance Sheet statements in a condensed form along with a summary of company news for the period.

READING AN ANNUAL REPORT

When reading an annual report, it is important to realize that the report will attempt to emphasize profitable prospects and play down reverses. From management's point of view, an annual report gives the company an opportunity to influence stockholders, company employees, the public, and financial advisors.

Current annual reports of major companies are well designed, often interesting, and easy to read. Typically, a letter from the president or a feature story reviews the operations for the past year and discusses the future prospects—the company's program for expansion and its research and development. The report may also present illustrations, charts, graphs, and pictures of company products, personnel, and activities.

Authorities require that the letter from the president be consistent with the financial data presented in the report. However, while reading the letter, be alert to pick up vague expressions concealing concern over business conditions; such as "we were heartened by an increase in the order rates;" "we regard this as a temporary situation;" "this is a year of transition;" or "our industrial operations are strengthening;" "agriculture is making a strong comeback;" "we expect to return to a growth position;" or "the important consumer segment has a positive outlook."

An annual report may also tell about the people who run the company; their pay and background; where they live; what they do; what the company does for employee welfare, such as insurance and hospitalization coverage and recreational facilities.

The annual report may explain company research, new products, and promotion and advertising policy. It may also tell how national, international and local economic situations affect its management policies.

The heart of an annual report is of course management's analysis of operations and the financial statements presented in the report. These include a Balance Sheet, Statements of Income, a Statement of Accumulated Retained Earnings, and a Statement of Changes in Financial Position. The techniques of reading and analyzing these important statements have been discussed in prior chapters.

Companies subject to SEC rules must show a *management's analysis of operating results* during the last two fiscal years. In some cases, an analysis may cover a larger period.

READING THE FINE PRINT

Pay attention to the fine print. Information in footnotes often affects the weight to be given to the report.

Look for footnotes reporting contingencies that might affect the company prospects, such as the possibility of additional income taxes being assessed for prior years; pending lawsuits which, if the company loses, may require the payment of substantial damages; renegotiation proceedings that may either give the corporation more income or force it to pay out substantial amounts.

Also check for these points:

Accounting methods used by the firm. Pay attention to the way inventories are valued. During periods of rising prices, the firm may use the LIFO method which assumes that the most recently acquired items are added to inventory and sold first. Consequently, higher values are assigned to inventories in cost of goods sold. This increases costs and reduces income. It also results in lower inventory values on the Balance Sheet.

Depreciation methods. The election of accelerated rates will reduce reported earnings; slower rates will tend to increase reported earnings.

Details of long-term debt for the type of security given for the debt and maturity dates. If in the near future the company must pay off its debt, this data will clue you into the company's needs for funds.

How the assets are valued. An item may be valued at cost but be worth much less—or much more—at the present time.

Events that happened after the close of the accounting year and their possible effect in modifying what is reported in the Balance Sheet. Disclosure of later events may appear in four places in the annual report. You might find them in the president's letter that accompanies the report, in the statements themselves, in footnotes to the statement, or in the auditor's report.

Payments of large debts soon after the close of the year and arranging for a new line of credit; the start of a law suit or tax action against the company or decision in a lawsuit after the close of the year; receipt of a large refund of taxes soon after the close of the year. Check for new commitments or expansion of facilities purchased and arranged for early delivery in the following year.

Trends shown on the five- or ten-year summaries of financial data. These will show in capsule form how well the company has done in increasing sales, controlling costs, and providing a better return on company assets. A steady growth pattern is an encouraging sign of future growth.

If the company has unfunded pension liabilities, these may be substantial and affect the company's financial commitments for other purposes.

Auditor's opinion, to see whether any qualifications have been made.

Long-term lease commitments. Contractual amounts of minimum annual lease payments are reported within the period over which the outlays will be made. Financial analysts review the minimum annual lease rentals to estimate "fixed charges" which the company must make. The value of leased property is listed as assets only if the lease contract is in substance an installment purchase.

Adjustments for inflation. The way inflationary adjustments affect a particular company's financial report depends on the interaction of income and expense items which are adjusted. Accounting for inflation is discussed later in this chapter.

Market price per share data. This data may be presented for several periods for comparison purposes.

Capital stock information. Treasury stock, stock options—warrants, common, and preferred shares out-standing; earnings per share; dividends per share.

Business segment and geographic area information.

10-K REPORT

The most extensive reports available to the public are the 10-K reports filed with the SEC. Copies may be requested from the company. The address for such a request is printed at the end of a company annual report.

The SEC requires large corporations to include in 10-K statements the cost of current replacement costs for inventory and productive capacity (plant and equipment). The 10-K must show how depreciation and the cost of goods sold would be affected if the Balance Sheet were recalculated on a replacement cost basis.

ACCOUNTING FOR INFLATION

Accounting rules developed during periods of relative economic stability. However, the unprecedented post-war inflationary period has confronted the accounting profession with the dilemma of how to adjust financial statements, which are based on "historical costs," to reflect changes in the general price levels. A historical cost is simply what was originally paid for an asset, and from your own personal experience, you know the effects of inflation. You know that a house bought 25 years ago for $25,000 may now be worth over $200,000. Thus, its historical cost of $25,000 fails to reflect its real value. Further, the dollar used to buy the house 25 years ago had a different purchasing power than the purchasing power of the current dollar. Now, if you add to this one example several thousand other items of property that a company may own, and which were bought at different periods, you can visualize the extent of the problem of accounting for inflation. However, recognizing the problem is a long way from finding a solution, and the accounting profession is not of one mind in providing one. Accountants have differing opinions of how to account for inflation and the significance of such reports.

Currently, accounting authorities require publicly held companies to adjust inventories, property, plant and equipment, and net income for inflation. Two methods of doing so are the constant dollar and current cost methods.

CONSTANT DOLLAR. This method uses the Consumer Price Index for all Urban Consumers (CPI-U) to restate amounts in the financial statements in terms of the general purchasing power of the dollar. Under the Constant Dollar method, original cost figures for property, plant, and equipment are adjusted for the CPI-U and depreciated using the same methods and useful lives used in the financial statement.

CURRENT COST. This method uses current values for specific assets used by the company to estimate replacement costs in current dollars for the inventories and property, and plant and equipment. Depreciation expense and cost of sales are restated based on the estimated replacement values.

Recent acquisition costs, data prepared by industry groups, or other similar sources, are used to estimate current costs of plant and equipment.

There are no adjustments under either method to present reduction of costs or increase in efficiencies from replacement of existing facilities.

Income taxes are the same as reported in the primary financial statements.

Monetary assets, cash, and claims to cash are also adjusted for inflation. During inflationary periods, monetary assets decline in value while holding liabilities is considered beneficial because they will be paid off with "cheaper dollars." For example, a company holding more monetary assets than monetary liabilities will show a decrease in purchasing power.

The way inflationary adjustments affect a particular company financial report depends on its interaction of income and expense items which are adjusted. Companies with rapid turnover and with low inventories in relation to sales are less affected by inflationary adjustments than companies with expensive, slower moving inventory. Companies that hold substantial receivables show general price-level losses. Companies that finance their operations more heavily with debt profit more from inflation than companies which rely on equity financing. However, price-level gains on debt financing are offset by increasing interest rates.

CHAPTER 6

SAMPLE ANALYSIS OF AN ANNUAL REPORT

=========

In the following pages, you will find the annual report of the Alberto-Culver Company for the fiscal year ended September 30, 1983. Its stock sells on the New York Stock Exchange and we will analyze its operations by applying the tests of the previous chapters.

As a preliminary, this summary of company operations may help you begin.

The Alberto-Culver Company has both foreign and domestic operations in three business units.

1. "'Mass Marketed Personal Use Products." This, the largest unit, provides approximately 62% of the net sales. It develops, manufactures, promotes and markets products for home consumption, such as items like shoes and boots, handbags, hair care products, and cleansing products.

2. "Institutional and Industrial Products." This unit accounts for approximately 21% of net sales, manufacturing specialty foods for institutions and restaurants, professional hair products such as hair sprays sold to beauty and barber salons, and cleaning aid products used by institutions and industries.

3. "Other Products." This unit accounts for approximately 17% of the sales. It sells professional beauty and barber products through company-operated wholesale outlet stores.

We suggest that you first briefly review the annual report on the following pages and then follow the analysis starting on page 103.

SAMPLE ANALYSIS OF AN ANNUAL REPORT

Chairman's Message

I am pleased to report that record earnings for the fourth quarter of our 1983 fiscal year showed that, as the country began to recover from a recession, Alberto-Culver was able to rebound from a downturn earlier in the year. Net earnings for the quarter accounted for more than half of the $3,909,000 in net earnings for the fiscal year, down from $6,601,000 for 1982. Sales for the year were down approximately two percent, dropping from $320,387,000 to $313,720,000.

Our results for the year were a disruption in steady growth marked by six consecutive years of increased sales and earnings. However, sales for fiscal 1983 would have been higher by $21.5 million and earnings would have been higher by $3.5 million or 90 cents a share if foreign exchange rates had remained the same as they were during the previous year. The unfavorable exchange rates masked the fact that our international operations actually performed exceptionally well.

Toiletries, our core business, had an excellent year. Our Professional Division did well, but was affected by the slow economic recovery. Sally Beauty Company enjoyed uninterrupted expansion and is now accelerating the opening of new wholesale beauty supply outlets.

Mrs. Dash, an innovative salt alternative introduced by the Household/Grocery Products Division in June, has been well received by consumers. This promising new product represents a new market for Alberto-Culver. The division was down, however, because of an unanticipated sharp drop in sales of Mr. Culver's Sparklers air fresheners and the introductory costs relating to Mrs. Dash.

Losses in our two leather goods subsidiaries were a major factor in the year's disappointing results, but we believe they will soon return to profitability. Operating efficiencies have been established in these subsidiaries and throughout the corporation, and new managers are now in key positions in the toiletries, household/grocery products and leather goods operations. An acquisition recently completed in Europe will increase our participation in the professional hair care industry and strengthen our presence in European markets.

With capable people in place, and strong advertising and promotion backing both new and existing products, I am optimistic about the coming year and Alberto-Culver's prospects for long-term growth.

Leonard N. Lavin

Leonard H. Lavin
Chairman, President, Chief Executive Officer
November 14, 1983

1

International

Alberto-Culver's international operations grew substantially during the fiscal year. Sales after translation to U.S. dollars were higher than in any previous year in the company's history despite unfavorable foreign exchange rates. Sales in local currencies in most major countries were up compared to the previous year. This growth is attributed to the success of new products, strong marketing and restructured operations in many countries.

The bulk of Alberto-Culver's business outside the United States and Canada is in hair care. Many products are tailored to meet specific cultural and physical hair care needs of the countries where they are introduced, but others have worldwide appeal. Most of the company's newer products are positioned for the upscale and fashion-oriented segment of foreign populations, the frequent users who prefer the quality of premium priced personal care items.

Alberto-Culver products are available in more than 100 countries or geographic regions, but the company derives a sizable portion of its sales from the countries where it has its own manufacturing, research and sales operations—England, Mexico, Puerto Rico, Canada and Australia.

Sales in the United Kingdom were up significantly, with a strong performance coming from the Alberto Jojoba line of shampoos and moisturizing conditioners during its first full marketing year. A new Camomile Care line was added in 1983 to further enhance Alberto-Culver's position as the market leader for shampoos and conditioners in the United Kingdom. Under the Jojoba and Camomile Care brand names, 15 items have been introduced in the United Kingdom and six in Australia. These lines will be expanded into other countries as well.

Puerto Rico, which distributes products throughout the Caribbean region, was a major contributor to the division's profits. Mexico achieved substantial growth that will make a notable contribution to corporate results when currency exchange rates stabilize.

Alberto Jojoba, formulated for the British market in June 1982, exceeded sales expectations and strengthened the company's position as the market leader for shampoos and conditioners in the United Kingdom.

2

SAMPLE ANALYSIS OF AN ANNUAL REPORT

A solid performance from smaller regions such as Taiwan and Scandinavia, where Alberto-Culver has a strong market position, helped contribute to earnings increases in fiscal 1983.

The International Division has made operating adjustments and improvements in certain areas where it has joint ventures, distributorships and licensing arrangements. It is closely evaluating the market potential of countries where the company currently does not have a presence.

In November of 1983, the company signed an agreement to acquire Indola Cosmetics B.V., a Dutch firm that markets hair care products to the professional hairdressing trade primarily in Europe. It also markets equipment and furniture for beauty salons. This business is expected to add to the division's sales and profits and strengthen its presence in European markets.

Toiletries

Fiscal 1983 was a very good year for Alberto-Culver's Toiletries Division. This division markets hair spray,

shampoo, conditioner, feminine deodorant, hairdressing and other toiletries. Sales increased on the overall strength of the division and good performances from several new products and line extensions. The company was able to generate profits from the division while reinvesting in new toiletry products and programs that should lead to continuing growth in 1984.

Sales of Alberto VO5 Shampoo increased significantly compared to the previous year, which also had been a year of impressive growth. Two formulas, Essence of Jojoba and Extra Body, contributed to the product's success in 1983, their first full year as part of the line. While the market is crowded, it is one of the largest categories in the health and beauty aids industry.

Sales exceeded expectations for the Alberto VO5 Instant Conditioners that debuted just prior to the beginning of the 1983 fiscal year.

3

85

Four formulas—Normal, Extra Body, Essence of Neutral Henna and Essence of Jojoba— were designed as companions to the company's successful shampoo line and have a unique triple conditioning action.

FDS Feminine Deodorant Spray, by far the leader in its category, sold particularly well in the second half of the fiscal year on the strength of two additional formulas, Baby Powder and Vinegar and Water, which accounted for more than 25 percent of the line's sales for the year.

Alberto VO5 Hair Spray, the division's best selling product and a market leader, overcame the impact of several competitive entries from the previous year and regained its share of what has become a larger market. The product's improved Crystal Clear formula does not leave a dull film on the hair as most hair sprays do. A comparison against leading competitive hair sprays is convincingly demonstrated in a new commercial.

The division will continue giving strong support to its existing products, and plans to add line extensions, reformulations and new products in 1984.

Household/Grocery

The Household/Grocery Products Division, which strives to develop and market innovative products that satisfy broad consumer needs not being met by existing products, introduced a salt alternative in June called Mrs. Dash. A blend of 14 herbs and spices and other natural ingredients, the product was well received by consumers because of its good taste as well as its health benefits. Mrs. Dash is virtually free of sodium and, unlike existing salt substitutes, has no chemical additives and contains virtually no potassium. Its market potential includes the vast number of Americans who are attempting to reduce their consumption of sodium, which has been linked to hypertension and heart problems.

Consumer health concerns about sodium have contributed to steady increases in sales of Mrs. Dash, a flavorful alternative to salt introduced nationwide in June.

4

SAMPLE ANALYSIS OF AN ANNUAL REPORT

After only four months on the market, Mrs. Dash was carried by more than 80 percent of all U.S. grocery outlets, and sales were meeting expectations as extensive advertising, couponing, sampling programs, refund offers and other measures alerted consumers to the availability of the product and its advantages over existing salt substitutes.

Mr. Culver's Sparklers, a decorative solid air freshener launched in 1981, suffered a severe drop in sales in 1983. Research determined that consumers were keeping Sparklers for their decorative appeal rather than repurchasing after the product's air freshening qualities were gone.

SugarTwin sugar substitute held up well against new competition. While its market share declined, the size of the market grew substantially. The product continues to hold a comfortable margin as the leading sugar substitute in Canada. Reformulated in 1982 to taste even more like sugar, it continues to appeal to consumers because of its flavor, competitively low cost and versatile use in baking or on the table.

Last year's unseasonably mild winter lowered sales of Static Guard anti-cling spray. Product movement is expected to increase with normal winter weather. Marketing activities for Static Guard and another innovative product, Baker's Joy flour and oil spray, are aimed at increasing consumer awareness of the availability of the products and their unique applications.

5

HOW TO READ A FINANCIAL STATEMENT

Professional

The Professional Division, which makes hair care products for professional beauty and barber salons, has shown an impressive record of sales and earnings for more than ten years. In 1983, the division performed well, although the sluggish economy affected the entire beauty industry and hindered the anticipated growth of the division. In fiscal 1984, an improving economy and new products should add sales and profits to its lines.

The TCB and VO5 Imperial lines are designed to meet the hair care needs of Blacks and Hispanics. This market segment had been rapidly outpacing the rest of the industry, but in 1983 was affected by the recession. While growth has given rise to numerous competitors, TCB continues to be one of the category leaders and innovators. TCB No Lye No Mix Relaxer debuted during the year as the first no lye relaxer that does not need to be mixed. Relaxers that must be mixed cannot be stored after mixing, causing waste. It was widely promoted nationwide through educational seminars for hairdressers and a program benefiting and co-sponsored by the United Negro College Fund. Contributions and support to educational, cultural and health programs are part of an ongoing major commitment to the Black community.

The new relaxer was supported by a companion product, Botanical Shampoo, the only shampoo on the market created specifically for use with no lye relaxers. It is formulated to neutralize and detangle hair in one step.

The TRESemme hair care line had its best year, with strong sales coming from the 4 + 4 Permanent Wave launched the year before. Line extensions for 4 + 4 included a styling glaze and a hair spray. TRESemme European Styling Mousse was introduced after the end of the year to benefit from the growing popularity of styling foams, a new product category for the division.

Consort maintained its position as one of the leading hair sprays for men. The Consort line is introducing a shampoo, a conditioner and a styling mousse, all targeted for male consumers.

6

SAMPLE ANALYSIS OF AN ANNUAL REPORT

In the coming year, the Professional Division will enhance its reputation as an authority on hair treatment by sponsoring more educational seminars and publishing literature for salon operators on news, trends and techniques. Advertising will be increased to inform hairdressers and salon patrons of the quality and value of the division's products.

Sally Beauty

Sally Beauty Company is the nation's largest wholesaler of beauty and barber supplies which it sells through store outlets located principally in shopping centers in the sunbelt states. Sally stores operate on the same concept as a supermarket, selling beauty products manufactured by hundreds of companies in the beauty field on a cash-and-carry basis. This profitable enterprise has grown quickly and consistently,

expanding through its existing business, acquisitions and new store openings. It opened 26 stores in fiscal year 1983 for a total of 145 in operation at the end of the year. The company expects to open approximately one new outlet per week during fiscal 1984.

Leather Goods

While sales of Frye boots and Phillippe handbags continued to be depressed, operating efficiencies have been implemented, and new designs have been well received by both the trade and consumers.

John A. Frye Shoe Company, Inc., after several years of excellent growth and profitability, was beset by a combination of difficulties including fashion changes, modified consumer spending, strong domestic and foreign competition and mild weather.

7

The company has reduced capacity and overhead, and has introduced new styles that reflect current fashion trends. The new lines are distinguished by soft leather and by lighter-weight soles for a refined, sleek look. Frye's traditional boots for men and women have been made more comfortable with softer leathers and new Frye Flex leather soles that are specially treated to feel broken in.

An exclusive new color, burnt cherry, has been very popular in boots as well as Frye's hand-sewn shoes. Frye is expanding its participation in the sizable shoe market, and is developing concept shops in department stores that display a broad range of Frye merchandise.

Phillippe of California, Inc., has upgraded its sales force and its styles of leather handbags in order to increase volume. A new line made of Belgian linen is being introduced in 1984 to diversify the product line and interest more stores in carrying Phillippe products. With the opening of a new showroom in Chicago, the company now reaches buyers through showrooms in four major cities across the country. Print ads in national magazines are helping to develop extensive consumer awareness of the classic styles and functional design of Phillippe's handbags.

Food Service

The Food Service Division recorded the highest sales in its history. Milani Food Service, the largest of three separate operations within the division, increased the size of its sales force and combined creative incentives with an innovative approach to marketing, resulting in wider penetration of restaurants, hospitals, schools and other food service markets. Nearly 50 new products were added to its line of more than 400 food bases, soups, dressings, sauces and desserts.

Milani Food Service also sells Mrs. Dash, the company's new salt alternative, in bottles as well as in individual portion packets. Mrs. Dash is also marketed by Alberto-Culver Food Service, a separate operation that uses brokers to reach distributors and chain accounts with volume quantities of the company's nationally

8

advertised branded products. Sales of SugarTwin sugar substitute by Alberto-Culver Food Service continued to rise despite new competition.

Milani Specialty Foods, formed by the division in 1982, distributes a small line of retail products, including Milani 1890 Salad Dressings, directly to grocery outlets. Milani Hot & Hearty Hot Broth Drink, a low-calorie, caffeine-free alternative to coffee and tea, was introduced at the close of the fiscal year. A second new retail product, Milani Liquid Bouillon, will be reaching grocery shelves in early 1984.

Masury-Columbia

Masury-Columbia Company, prominent in floor maintenance chemicals and equipment for department stores, schools, service centers and other chain accounts, developed and introduced a new line for a segment of the industry that is growing faster than the company's traditional customer base.

The new line, called Crewmaster, includes 13 different products to meet 80 to 90 percent of

the chemical cleaning needs of professional contract maintenance firms. These firms are maintenance experts that require virtually no training from the Masury-Columbia sales force, but must depend upon superior floor strippers, cleaners and finishers to build their reputation.

The Crewmaster line meets their requirements and is selling exceptionally well, particularly a high-speed floor finish. The same technology used to develop this product was applied to a new product for the company's traditional line. Called Paragon/VHS, it can withstand the high speed buffing necessary to create the shiny wet-look now preferred by retailers and other clients.

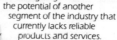

Masury-Columbia plans to build upon its Crewmaster line and improve the distribution of its Finnell cleaning machinery. It is also investigating the potential of another segment of the industry that currently lacks reliable products and services.

9

HOW TO READ A FINANCIAL STATEMENT

Consolidated Statements of Earnings
Alberto-Culver Company and Subsidiaries

	Year ended September 30,		
	1983	1982	1981
Net sales	**$313,719,923**	320,386,783	294,368,879
Costs and expenses:			
Cost of products sold	**154,425,773**	161,433,077	150,987,564
Advertising, promotion, selling and administrative	**147,514,240**	144,139,352	128,367,321
Total costs and expenses	**301,940,013**	305,572,429	279,354,885
Operating profit	**11,779,910**	14,814,354	15,013,994
Other expense (income):			
Interest expense	**6,640,912**	6,375,807	3,903,579
Other, net	**127,386**	(632,993)	93,767
Total other expense (income)	**6,768,298**	5,742,814	3,997,346
Earnings before income taxes	**5,011,612**	9,071,540	11,016,648
Provision for income taxes (note 9)	**1,103,000**	2,471,000	4,994,000
Net earnings	**$ 3,908,612**	6,600,540	6,022,648
Net earnings per share	**$1.01**	1.73	1.56

See accompanying notes to consolidated financial statements.

Consolidated Statements of Retained Earnings
Alberto-Culver Company and Subsidiaries

	Year ended September 30,		
	1983	1982	1981
Retained earnings, beginning of year	**$69,516,237**	64,804,573	60,324,924
Net earnings	**3,908,612**	6,600,540	6,022,648
	73,424,849	71,405,113	66,347,572
Less cash dividends—$.54 per share in 1983; $.50 per share in 1982; $.40 per share in 1981	**(2,078,076)**	(1,888,876)	(1,542,999)
Retained earnings, end of year	**$71,346,773**	69,516,237	64,804,573

See accompanying notes to consolidated financial statements.

10

SAMPLE ANALYSIS OF AN ANNUAL REPORT

Consolidated Balance Sheets
Alberto-Culver Company and Subsidiaries

Assets	September 30	
	1983	1982
Current Assets:		
Cash		
Short-term investments	$ 3,085,628	2,852,320
Receivables, less allowance for doubtful accounts	596,754	562,069
(1983—$1,557,000; 1982—$1,755,000)		
Inventories (note 3)	59,533,065	61,472,626
Prepaid expenses	63,796,988	64,318,348
	3,640,991	2,601,633
Total current assets	130,653,426	131,806,996
Property, plant and equipment, net (notes 4, 5 and 10)	28,480,313	28,525,257
Goodwill, net	7,184,630	7,412,707
Other assets, net	6,668,929	7,269,978
	$172,987,298	175,014,938

Liabilities and Stockholders' Equity		
Current liabilities:		
Short-term borrowings		
Current maturities of long-term debt	$ 33,429,209	31,228,618
Accounts payable	1,661,532	3,547,454
Accrued expenses:	30,746,621	36,875,802
Compensation and payroll taxes		
Promotional allowances	3,843,803	3,486,513
Other	4,727,102	5,558,684
Income taxes	4,549,484	4,818,719
	780,039	1,379,890
Total current liabilities	79,737,790	86,895,680
Long-term debt (note 5)	20,886,261	18,918,688
Deferred income taxes (note 9)	3,490,266	1,916,463
Stockholders' equity:		
Common stock without par value; stated value		
of $.22 per share. Authorized 7,000,000 shares;		
issued 4,774,456 shares	1,061,109	1,061,109
Additional paid-in capital	8,323,625	8,329,599
Retained earnings	71,346,773	69,516,237
Foreign currency translation	(2,695,790)	(2,400,364)
	78,035,717	76,506,581
Less treasury stock, at cost (924,085 shares in 1983		
and 930,110 shares in 1982)	9,162,736	9,222,474
Total stockholders' equity	68,872,981	67,284,107
	$172,987,298	175,014,938

See accompanying notes to consolidated financial statements.

11

HOW TO READ A FINANCIAL STATEMENT

Consolidated Statements of Changes in Financial Position
Alberto-Culver Company and Subsidiaries

| | Year ended September 30, | | |
	1983	1982	1981
Sources of working capital:			
Provided from operations:			
Net earnings	$ 3,908,612	6,600,540	6,022,648
Add charges (deduct income) not affecting working capital:			
Depreciation	3,590,558	3,216,538	3,036,959
Amortization of goodwill and other assets	1,027,552	1,250,287	760,207
Deferred income taxes	1,432,000	(27,000)	466,000
Gain on sales of property, plant and equipment	(337,153)	(316,617)	(2,992)
Other	(55,200)	(50,795)	(55,200)
Total provided from operations	9,566,369	10,672,953	10,227,622
Increase in long-term debt	15,071,836	12,970,000	7,105,075
Proceeds from disposals of property, plant and equipment	872,387	2,428,672	424,948
Proceeds from exercise of stock options	53,764	3,750	146,027
Treasury stock issued to employee benefit plans	—	899,971	—
Change in other assets	513,842	(1,127,091)	20,490
	26,078,198	25,848,255	17,924,162
Applications of working capital:			
Capital expenditures	4,217,488	9,017,713	8,883,515
Reduction in long-term debt	13,104,263	3,668,570	2,293,868
Net noncurrent assets of acquired companies	—	1,228,579	4,112,607
Cash dividends	2,078,076	1,888,876	1,542,999
Stock purchased for treasury	—	630,599	473,102
Additions to trade names and goodwill	666,812	503,482	749,349
Foreign currency translation excluding $288,187 in 1983 and $728,024 in 1982 not affecting working capital	7,239	1,672,340	—
	20,073,878	18,610,159	18,055,440
Increase (decrease) in working capital	$ 6,004,320	7,238,096	(131,278)
Increase (decrease) in components of working capital:			
Current assets:			
Cash and short-term investments	$ 267,993	168,528	238,219
Receivables	(1,939,561)	11,466,421	7,789,398
Inventories	(521,360)	11,940,531	9,326,662
Prepaid expenses	1,039,358	776,638	619,869
	(1,153,570)	24,352,118	17,974,148
Current liabilities:			
Short-term borrowings and current maturities of long-term debt	314,669	15,729,667	12,568,810
Accounts payable and accrued expenses	(6,872,708)	2,181,948	7,822,233
Income taxes	(599,851)	(797,593)	(2,285,617)
	(7,157,890)	17,114,022	18,105,426
Increase (decrease) in working capital	$ 6,004,320	7,238,096	(131,278)

See accompanying notes to consolidated financial statements.

12

SAMPLE ANALYSIS OF AN ANNUAL REPORT

Notes to Consolidated Financial Statements

(1) Summary of Significant Accounting Policies

PRINCIPLES OF CONSOLIDATION
The consolidated financial statements include accounts of the company and its subsidiaries. All intercompany accounts and transactions have been eliminated.

SHORT-TERM INVESTMENTS
Short-term investments are stated at cost, which approximates market.

INVENTORIES
Inventories are stated at the lower of cost (first-in, first-out method) or market.

PROPERTY, PLANT AND EQUIPMENT
Property, plant and equipment are carried at cost. Depreciation is provided primarily on the straight-line method based on estimated useful lives of the assets. Expenditures for maintenance and repairs are expensed as incurred.

GOODWILL
The cost of goodwill is amortized primarily over forty years.

PENSION PLANS
Normal service costs are accrued and funded currently. Prior service costs are amortized and funded over thirty years.

FOREIGN CURRENCY TRANSLATION
The company adopted the provisions of Financial Accounting Standards Board Statement No. 52 entitled "Foreign Currency Translation" in fiscal year 1982. Accordingly, foreign currency balance sheet accounts are generally translated at rates of exchange in effect at the balance sheet date. Results of operations are translated using the average exchange rates prevailing throughout the period. For fiscal 1981, depreciation and cost of sales were translated by the historical method.

Under Statement No. 52, translation effects for operations in countries which do not have hyperinflationary economies are recorded as foreign currency translation in stockholders' equity. Translation effects for operations in countries considered to be hyperinflationary and realized gains and losses from foreign currency transactions are included in net earnings for the period. In fiscal 1981, all translation effects were charged to operations.

The following is an analysis of changes in the foreign currency translation account:

	1983	1982
Balance, beginning of year	$ 2,400,364	396,489
Aggregate foreign currency translation adjustments, net of income taxes of $616,000 in 1982	295,426	2,003,875
Balance, end of year	$ 2,695,790	2,400,364

INCOME TAXES
Provision is made for deferred income taxes resulting from timing differences in the recognition of revenue and expense for tax and financial statement purposes. Investment tax credits are accounted for as a reduction of the provision for income taxes in the year the credits arise.

CALCULATION OF EARNINGS PER SHARE
Earnings per share are based on the weighted average shares outstanding during the year (1983—3,859,892; 1982—3,804,449; 1981—3,854,405).

(2) Foreign Operations

Net assets of the company's foreign operations are summarized below:

	1983	1982
Net current assets	$ 9,293,490	9,397,580
Net other assets, principally property, plant and equipment	2,210,981	1,798,350
	$11,504,471	11,195,930

Changes in the relationship between the U.S. dollar and foreign currencies resulted in exchange losses of $1,354,000 and $965,000 in 1983 and 1981, respectively. Foreign currency translation had an insignificant effect on earnings in 1982.

(3) Inventories

Inventories consist of the following:

	1983	1982
Finished goods	$40,018,162	40,897,909
Work-in-process	4,354,737	4,810,027
Raw materials	19,424,089	18,610,412
	$63,796,988	64,318,348

(4) Property, Plant and Equipment

Property, plant and equipment are classified as follows:

	1983	1982
Land	$ 1,947,010	2,036,816
Buildings	17,255,775	16,179,973
Machinery and equipment	34,580,094	33,689,359
	53,782,879	51,906,148
Less accumulated depreciation	25,302,566	23,380,891
	$28,480,313	28,525,257

13

Notes Continued

(5) Long-Term Debt

Long-term debt, exclusive of current maturities, consists of the following:

	1983	1982
Installment notes payable:		
10% due March, 1985	$ 625,000	625,000
10% due February, 1986	340,000	510,000
10% due July, 1986	1,800,000	2,700,000
10% due April, 1987	1,200,000	1,600,000
11% due March, 1988	133,334	165,944
10% mortgage note due October, 2003	303,864	313,260
Industrial development bonds:		
6.75% due October, 1984	300,000	300,000
13% due September, 1991	—	1,400,000
12.25% due December, 1991	973,119	971,336
11% note due December, 1985	15,000,000	—
Revolving credit note	—	10,000,000
Capitalized leases at weighted average interest rate of 13% in 1983 and 14% in 1982	210,944	328,784
Other	—	4,364
	$20,886,261	18,918,688

Maturities of long-term debt for the next five years are as follows: 1984—$1,662,000; 1985—$2,581,000; 1986—$16,578,000; 1987—$451,000; 1988—$47,000.

Land, buildings and other assets with a net book value of $2,718,000 at September 30, 1983 are pledged under various loan agreements.

The company entered into a $50 million revolving credit agreement with several banks in 1982. Borrowings may be obtained, at the company's option, at the prevailing prime interest rate or at a certain percentage above the London Interbank Offered Rate (LIBOR) or the certificate of deposit rate. There were no borrowings under this agreement at September 30, 1983.

Various borrowing arrangements impose restrictions on such items as total debt, working capital, dividend payments, treasury stock purchases and interest expense. At September 30, 1983, the company was in compliance with these arrangements and $33.1 million of consolidated retained earnings was not restricted as to the payment of dividends and purchases of treasury stock.

In addition to the revolving credit agreement, the company had unused lines of credit of $49.5 million with various banks at September 30, 1983. The credit lines, which required no compensating balances, may be terminated at the option of the banks or the company.

(6) Stock Option Plan

In January, 1977, stockholders approved the employee nonqualified stock option plan which authorizes issuance of options to purchase not more than 150,000 shares of the company's common stock at a price not less than the fair market value of the stock at the date of grant. In October, 1981, the company amended the plan retroactively to provide for the granting of incentive stock options and to permit conversion of outstanding nonqualified options to incentive stock options. Options expire five years from date of grant and become exercisable on a cumulative basis in four equal annual increments commencing one year after the date of grant.

Shares under option at September 30, 1983 are summarized below:

Year Granted	Shares Under Option	Per Share Option Price	Total Option Price
1979	500	$7.63 to 7.88	$ 3,875
1980	4,025	8.31 to 9.44	34,494
1981	11,550	13.25	153,038
1982	16,400	12.75	209,100
1983	22,600	21.81	492,906
	55,075		$893,413

Options for 6,025 shares were exercised in 1983 whereas options for 500 shares were exercised in the prior year. During 1983 and 1982, options for 5,675 and 5,100 shares, respectively, were terminated. Options for 12,725 shares were exercisable at September 30, 1983.

(7) Treasury Stock and Additional Paid-In Capital

Changes in treasury stock and additional paid-in capital during 1983, 1982 and 1981 were as follows (in thousands):

	Treasury Stock		Additional Paid-In Capital
	Shares	Amount	
Balance at September 30, 1980	932	$9,069	$8,230
Stock options exercised	(21)	(205)	(58)
Stock purchased for treasury	43	474	—
Balance at September 30, 1981	954	9,338	8,172
Stock options exercised	(1)	(5)	(1)
Stock purchased for treasury	51	630	—
Shares issued to employee benefit plans	(74)	(741)	159
Balance at September 30, 1982	930	9,222	8,330
Stock options exercised	(6)	(59)	(6)
Balance at September 30, 1983	924	$9,163	$8,324

14

Notes Continued

(8) Pension Plans

The company has eight noncontributory pension plans for eligible employees. Pension expense for the years ended September 30, 1983, 1982 and 1981 was $363,500, $254,100 and $233,400, respectively. A comparison of accumulated plan benefits as of the beginning of the latest plan years is presented below:

	1983	1982
Actuarial present value of accumulated plan benefits:		
Vested	$ 970,533	840,661
Nonvested	148,892	122,450
	$1,119,425	963,111

Net plan assets of $1.4 million and $1.0 million were available for benefits at September 30, 1983 and 1982, respectively. The weighted average assumed rate of return used in determining the actuarial present value of accumulated plan benefits was approximately 8.0% for 1983 and 1982.

(9) Income Taxes

The provision for income taxes consists of the following:

	1983	1982	1981
Currently payable:			
Federal	$(1,393,000)	166,000	2,709,000
Foreign	1,064,000	2,012,000	1,194,000
State	—	320,000	625,000
	(329,000)	2,498,000	4,528,000
Deferred:			
Federal	1,183,000	(38,000)	498,000
Foreign	249,000	11,000	(32,000)
	1,432,000	(27,000)	466,000
	$ 1,103,000	2,471,000	4,994,000

The deferred income tax provision includes the following components:

	1983	1982	1981
Accelerated tax depreciation	$ 697,000	402,000	317,000
Gain on sale of assets	—	(241,000)	—
DISC income	133,000	109,000	229,000
Foreign tax credit carry-over	(190,000)	—	—
Promotion accruals	721,000	(143,000)	(101,000)
Prepaid expenses	(170,000)	186,000	—
Other	241,000	(340,000)	21,000
	$1,432,000	(27,000)	466,000

The difference between the effective income tax rate on earnings for financial statement purposes and the United States statutory federal income tax rate is summarized below:

	1983	1982	1981
Statutory tax rate	46.0%	46.0%	46.0%
Effect of foreign income tax rates	(5.9)	(3.3)	(.8)
State income taxes, net of federal tax benefit	—	1.9	3.4
Investment and other tax credits	(7.0)	(12.4)	(4.3)
Adjustment of prior years taxes	(10.8)	(4.3)	—
Other, net	(.3)	(.7)	1.0
Effective tax rate	22.0%	27.2%	45.3%

Domestic earnings before income taxes were $1.7 million, $4.9 million and $11.0 million in 1983, 1982 and 1981, respectively. Foreign earnings before income taxes were $3.3 million, $4.2 million and $53 thousand in 1983, 1982 and 1981, respectively.

Undistributed earnings of the company's international operations are intended to remain permanently invested to finance future growth and expansion. Accordingly, no U.S. income taxes have been provided on those earnings which aggregated $13,078,000 at September 30, 1983. Should such earnings be distributed the credit for foreign income taxes paid would substantially offset applicable U.S. income taxes.

(10) Lease Commitments

The company's principal leases cover manufacturing and warehousing properties, office facilities, wholesale outlet stores, data processing equipment and automobiles. At September 30, 1983, future minimum payments under noncancellable leases are as follows:

	Capital Leases	Operating Leases
1984	$176,047	4,846,452
1985	157,620	3,936,466
1986	65,848	3,020,514
1987	4,508	2,079,123
1988	—	1,219,617
1989 and later	—	1,514,307
Total minimum lease payments	404,023	16,616,479
Minimum sublease rental income	—	(208,984)
Net minimum lease payments	404,023	16,407,495
Less interest	(48,580)	
Present value of net minimum lease payments	$355,443	

Capital leases included in the consolidated balance sheets at September 30, 1983 and 1982 are summarized below:

	1983	1982
Machinery and equipment	$654,005	654,615
Accumulated depreciation and amortization	316,112	297,171
Obligations under capital leases:		
Current	144,499	144,907
Long-term	210,944	328,784

Certain leases require the company to pay real estate taxes, insurance, maintenance and special assessments.

Total rental expense for operating leases amounted to $7,453,000 in 1983, $6,756,000 in 1982 and $4,904,000 in 1981.

15

Notes Continued

(11) Business Segments and Geographic Area Information

The principal business of Alberto-Culver Company and its subsidiaries is developing, manufacturing, promoting and marketing products which are designed for sale at retail and ultimately for personal use or use in the home (referred to as "mass marketed personal use products").

Another segment of the company's business is "institutional and industrial products" which includes items such as specialty foods for institutions and restaurants, professional hair care products sold to beauty and barber distributors and cleaning aid products intended for end-use by institutions and industries.

The "other products" business segment principally represents the company's and other manufacturers' professional beauty and barber products sold through company operated wholesale outlet stores. This segment also includes contract packaging services performed for other companies which are provided through the company's own production facilities.

Segment and geographic data for the years ended September 30, 1983, 1982 and 1981 are as follows:

Business Segments Information	1983	1982	1981
Net sales:			
Mass marketed personal use products	$196,674,249	208,241,390	213,990,940
Institutional and industrial products	68,205,728	75,419,302	61,633,767
Other products	55,034,042	42,365,335	20,575,596
Eliminations	(6,194,096)	(5,639,244)	(1,831,424)
	$313,719,923	320,386,783	294,368,879
Earnings before income taxes:			
Operating profit:			
Mass marketed personal use products	$ 810,937	1,111,962	7,861,388
Institutional and industrial products	11,899,701	13,949,948	9,653,976
Other products	3,570,234	2,638,699	440,413
	16,280,872	17,700,609	17,955,777
Unallocated expenses, net	(4,628,348)	(2,253,262)	(3,035,550)
Interest expense	(6,640,912)	(6,375,807)	(3,903,579)
	$ 5,011,612	9,071,540	11,016,648
Identifiable assets:			
Mass marketed personal use products	$111,909,884	116,139,772	99,833,340
Institutional and industrial products	28,181,372	25,797,859	24,585,154
Other products	25,586,099	26,265,082	17,517,612
Corporate	7,229,943	6,812,225	4,026,854
	$172,907,298	175,014,938	145,962,960
Depreciation and amortization expense:			
Mass marketed personal use products	$ 2,947,220	2,988,615	2,663,503
Institutional and industrial products	528,958	456,766	439,039
Other products	855,275	686,626	386,918
Corporate	286,657	334,818	307,706
	$ 4,618,110	4,466,825	3,797,166
Capital expenditures:			
Mass marketed personal use products	$ 2,735,842	3,969,090	5,408,801
Institutional and industrial products	469,679	504,705	440,886
Other products	909,513	450,909	463,379
Corporate	2,454	4,093,009	2,570,449
	$ 4,217,488	9,017,713	8,883,515

Geographic Area Information			
Net sales:			
United States	$263,691,004	271,159,831	245,796,978
Foreign	52,364,403	51,818,889	50,143,964
Eliminations	(2,335,404)	(2,591,937)	(1,572,063)
	$313,719,923	320,386,783	294,368,879
Operating profit:			
United States	$ 14,468,806	14,838,440	17,530,196
Foreign	1,812,066	2,862,169	425,581
	$ 16,280,872	17,700,609	17,955,777
Identifiable assets:			
United States	$142,313,374	146,726,881	119,356,746
Foreign	23,443,981	21,475,832	22,579,360
Corporate	7,229,943	6,812,225	4,026,854
	$172,907,298	175,014,938	145,962,960

"Unallocated expenses, net" principally consist of general corporate expenses and foreign exchange gains and losses. Corporate assets are
16 primarily cash and equipment

98

Notes Continued

(12) Quarterly Financial Data

Unaudited quarterly statement of earnings information for the years ended September 30, 1983 and 1982 are summarized below (in thousands, except per share amounts):

Quarter	Net Sales	Cost of Products Sold	Net Earnings	Earnings Per Share
1983				
First	$78,434	38,054	691	18
Second	76,591	37,003	186	05
Third	77,082	37,519	979	25
Fourth	81,613	41,850	2,053	53

Quarter	Net Sales	Cost of Products Sold	Net Earnings	Earnings Per Share
1982				
First	$81,037	40,256	1,460	38
Second	75,824	36,865	1,578	42
Third	79,106	39,381	1,642	43
Fourth	84,420	44,931	1,921	50

Accountants' Report

The Board of Directors and Stockholders
Alberto-Culver Company

We have examined the consolidated balance sheets of Alberto-Culver Company and subsidiaries as of September 30, 1983 and 1982 and the related consolidated statements of earnings, retained earnings and changes in financial position for each of the years in the three-year period ended September 30, 1983. Our examinations were made in accordance with generally accepted auditing standards and, accordingly, included such tests of the accounting records and such other auditing procedures as we considered necessary in the circumstances.

In our opinion, the aforementioned consolidated financial statements present fairly the financial position of Alberto-Culver Company and subsidiaries at September 30, 1983 and 1982 and the results of their operations and the changes in their financial position for each of the years in the three-year period ended September 30, 1983, in conformity with generally accepted accounting principles consistently applied during the period except for the change, with which we concur, in the method of accounting for foreign currency translation as described in note 1 of notes to consolidated financial statements.

Chicago, Illinois
November 14, 1983

Peat, Marwick, Mitchell & Co.

17

HOW TO READ A FINANCIAL STATEMENT

**Management's Discussion and Analysis of
Results of Operations and Financial Condition**

RESULTS OF OPERATIONS
The company's sales in 1983 were $313.7 million, a
decrease of 2.1% from sales of $320.4 million in 1982.
Sales in 1982 increased 8.8% compared to 1981.

"Mass marketed personal use products" sales were
$196.7 million in 1983 compared to $208.2 million in
1982. The company's Frye footwear and Phillippe
handbag product lines experienced lower sales primarily
due to the continuing effects of the economic recession,
strong domestic and foreign competition and fashion
changes. Sales of Mr. Culver's Sparklers, a solid air
freshener, declined sharply in 1983. Consumers retained
Sparklers for their decorative appeal rather than replacing
them after the air freshening qualities had dissipated.
Partially offsetting these sales declines were increases in
the company's toiletries and international operations.
Sales of mass marketed personal use products decreased
2.7% in 1982 compared to 1981.

Sales for the "institutional and industrial products"
business segment decreased 9.6% in 1983 compared to
1982. The principal factor for the decline was lower sales
of the professional division's TCB ethnic product line,
which was negatively affected by the recession and
increased competition. Sales of institutional and
industrial products increased 22.4% in 1982 compared
to 1981.

Total sales for the "other products" business segment
were $55.0 million in 1983 or 29.9% higher than the
prior year. Improved sales of existing wholesale outlet
stores plus the addition of 26 new wholesale outlet
stores for the distribution of the company's and other
manufacturers' beauty and barber supplies were the
principal reasons for the sales gains. Sales for the "other
products" category were $42.4 million in 1982
compared to $20.6 million in 1981. Business acquisitions
pertaining to the "other products" segment have been
included in the consolidated financial statements since
their dates of purchase in 1982 and 1981.

Cost of products sold as a percentage of sales decreased
in 1983 to 49.2% compared to 50.4% in 1982 and
51.3% in 1981. Variances between the periods are
principally due to changes in product sales mix, higher
selling prices and cost efficiencies.

The advertising, promotion, selling and administrative
expense category increased 2.3% in 1983 and 12.3% in
1982. During 1983, the company continued to make
substantial expenditures for advertising, promotion,
market research and new products development. In
addition, selling and administrative expenses rose
primarily due to the growth of the "other products"
business segment and the company's international
operations.

Interest expense increased 4.2% in 1983 compared to
an increase of 63.3% in 1982. The primary reason for the
increase in 1983 was higher borrowing levels related to
expenditures for fixed assets and working capital
requirements.

Changes in the "other, net" category in 1983, 1982 and
1981 primarily resulted from foreign currency translations.
The effect of foreign currency translation on the
company's earnings during this period is disclosed in
"note 2" to the consolidated financial statements.

Income tax provisions as a percentage of earnings before
income taxes were 22.0%, 27.2% and 45.3% in 1983,
1982 and 1981, respectively. The effective tax rate for
1983 was lower than the statutory tax rate primarily due
to adjustments of prior years' taxes, investment tax
credits and foreign income taxed at lower rates. The
lower effective tax rates for 1982 and 1981 were
substantially attributable to investment tax credits. Other
factors which influenced the effective tax rates for 1983,
1982 and 1981 are described in "note 9" to the
consolidated financial statements.

Net earnings in 1983 decreased to $3.9 million or $1.01
per share. Net earnings in 1982 were $6.6 million or
$1.73 per share versus 1981 earnings of $6.0 million or
$1.56 per share.

18

100

SAMPLE ANALYSIS OF AN ANNUAL REPORT

FINANCIAL CONDITION

The company continues to maintain a strong financial condition. During the period 1981 through 1983, operations were bolstered by business acquisitions, the introduction of new products and the company's investment in advertising and promotion to support its brands.

A continued commitment to its asset management programs is reflected in the company's current ratio increasing to 1.64 to 1.00 in 1983 from 1.54 to 1.00 in 1981. Working capital at September 30, 1983 was $50.9 million, an increase of $13.1 million or 34.7% for the three-year period. Working capital invested in receivables and inventories less accounts payable amounted to $92.6 million at September 30, 1983, which was $37.8 million greater than the comparable investment at the beginning of 1981. Since September 30, 1980, long-term debt rose $16.6 million and short-term borrowings, including current maturities of long-term debt, increased $28.6 million.

Expenditures for capital additions and funds paid for acquired companies totaled $29.8 million for the three years ended September 30, 1983. Additionally, the company purchased $1.1 million of its common stock and paid cash dividends of $5.5 million. Dividends per share were 54¢ in 1983 compared to 50¢ in 1982 and 40¢ in 1981.

At September 30, 1983, the company had available $50 million under its revolving credit agreement and $49.5 million of unused lines of credit with various banks.

INFLATION

The rate of inflation was high in 1981 and 1982; however, inflation declined significantly during 1983. During this three-year period, the company was able to increase its gross profit margin through favorable product sales mix, price increases and cost efficiencies.

The company is not required to report the effects of inflation under the criteria set forth in Statement No. 33 of the Financial Accounting Standards Board. However, using constant dollar accounting, net sales would have been $313.7 million, $327.0 million and $315.5 million in 1983, 1982 and 1981, respectively. It is estimated that 1983 net earnings would have been lower than reported if current costs had been used to compute inventories and depreciation. This decrease in earnings would have been offset in part by an unrealized gain on net monetary liabilities.

Market Price of Common Stock and Dividends Per Share
Alberto-Culver Company and Subsidiaries

The high and low sales prices of the company's common stock on the New York Stock Exchange and dividends per share paid in each quarter of fiscal years 1983 and 1982 are as follows:

| | Market Price Range | | | | Dividends Per Share | |
| | 1983 | | 1982 | | | |
	High	Low	High	Low	1983	1982
First Quarter	$24¼	12⅞	13¾	10½	$.135	.125
Second Quarter	20¼	16	14¼	11½	.135	.125
Third Quarter	18¾	14⅜	14¾	11	.135	.125
Fourth Quarter	17¼	13⅝	14⅜	10¾	.135	.125
					$.54	.50

Stockholders of record on November 18, 1983 totaled 2,411.

19

HOW TO READ A FINANCIAL STATEMENT

Selected Financial Data
Alberto-Culver Company and Subsidiaries

	1983	1982	1981	1980	1979
				Year ended September 30,	
Net sales	$313,719,923	320,386,783	294,368,879	229,261,194	187,927,162
Cost of products sold	154,425,773	161,433,077	150,987,564	117,250,330	91,081,454
Interest expense	6,640,912	6,375,807	3,903,579	1,645,333	936,248
Earnings before gain on sale of trademarks, income taxes and extraordinary gain	5,011,612	9,071,540	11,016,648	8,459,364	7,343,195
Provision for income taxes*	1,103,000	2,471,000	4,994,000	3,987,000	3,672,000
Earnings before gain on sale of trademarks and extraordinary gain*	3,908,612	6,600,540	6,022,648	4,472,364	3,671,195
Earnings per share before gain on sale of trademarks and extraordinary gain*	1.01	1.73	1.56	1.12	.88
Cash dividends per share	.54	.50	.40	.36	.36
Cash and short-term investments	3,682,382	3,414,389	3,245,861	3,007,642	3,576,679
Working capital	50,915,636	44,911,316	37,673,220	37,804,498	35,241,864
Current ratio	1.64 to 1	1.52 to 1	1.54 to 1	1.73 to 1	1.87 to 1
Property, plant and equipment, net	28,480,313	28,525,257	25,502,688	19,331,958	17,430,647
Total assets	172,987,298	175,014,938	145,962,960	117,906,217	98,140,711
Long-term debt	20,086,261	18,918,688	9,617,258	4,284,515	2,583,264
Stockholders' equity	68,872,981	67,284,107	64,699,685	60,547,111	53,936,141

*Earnings before gain on sale of trademarks and extraordinary gain are equivalent to net earnings for the respective year except for 1980 and 1979. In 1980, the sale of certain Japanese trademark rights resulted in a nonrecurring gain of $5,963,422 or $1.49 per share after deducting income taxes of $2,930,000 and other related costs. During 1979, the settlement of a lawsuit resulted in an extraordinary net gain of $2,128,576 or 51 cents per share. The nonrecurring gain and extraordinary gain are included in net earnings in the consolidated statement of earnings for the respective year.

Annual 10-K Report
Stockholders may obtain a copy of the company's 1983 Form 10-K Report filed with the Securities and Exchange Commission without charge by writing to the Corporate Secretary, Alberto-Culver Company, 2525 Armitage Avenue, Melrose Park, Illinois 60160

20

The first thing that you should have noticed in reviewing the report is the decline in sales. The message of the chairman attempts to minimize the sales decline by starting with an upbeat message: "I am pleased to report that record earnings for the fourth quarter . . . Alberto-Culver was able to rebound. . . ." Therefore, your first attention should be directed toward the Statement of Earnings to determine the trouble spots in the company lines and whether they are serious or temporary aberrations. In order to determine this it will be necessary to review several sections of the report. Data are scattered throughout the report and have to be selected and organized for analysis.

STATEMENT OF EARNINGS

A short Consolidated Statement of Earnings is printed on page 10 of the report. It briefly reports the operations for the last three fiscal years ended September 30, 1983, 1982 and 1981. For other details, you have to read (1) the Notes on page 16 under "Business Segments and Geographic Area Information," which gives a breakdown of sales according to the company operating units and (2) a company explanation of sales on pages 2 to 9. The serious nature of the data is softened by the decorative display of company products.

A steady decline in net sales was experienced by the "Mass Marketed Personal Use Products" segment from

1981 through 1983 after years of continuous growth prior to 1981. This is reflected in the business segment information on page 16 and the five-year summary of selected data on page 20 of the report. On pages 2 to 9, the company attributed the decline mainly to the economic recession, which resulted in decreased consumer spending and changing styles. The company explanation of the decline appears straight-forward and its expectation of a turnaround reasonable.

COST OF GOODS SOLD—INVENTORIES

In 1983, sales declined 2.1% and cost of goods sold declined 4.3%. On page 18 of the report, the company attributes this favorable relationship to higher selling prices and cost efficiencies.

Example—

		Percent
1982 Sales	$320,386,783	100.0
1983 Sales	313,719,923	97.9
Decline	6,666,860	2.1
1982 Cost of Goods Sold	161,433,077	100.0
1983 Cost of Goods Sold	154,425,773	95.7
Decline	$ 7,007,304	4.3

Inventory turnover. The inventory turnover has declined from 2.51 times per year in 1982 to 2.4 times per year in 1983.

Example—

Inventory turnover is calculated by dividing cost of goods sold by total average inventory.

$$1983 \text{ Turnover: } \frac{\$154,425,773}{(\$63,796,988 + \$64,318,348) \div 2} = 2.41$$

This change is too insignificant to be of concern. As the product mix is so varied, it is difficult to compare this rate to any industry standard without knowing the specific levels of inventory for each of the product lines.

SELLING EXPENSES

Management's discussion and analysis of results of operations and financial condition on page 18 of the report state that advertising, promotion, selling, and administrative expenses increased 2.3% in 1983 and 12.3% in 1982. As a percentage of net sales, the selling expenses have risen from 43.6% in 1981, to 45.0% in 1982, to 47.7% in 1983. The company claims that it has been making substantial expenditures for advertising, promotion, market research, and new product development in 1983 and 1982 and will continue to do so in order to increase sales volume.

OPERATING PROFIT

The 1983 operating profit was down 20.5% compared to a 1.3% decline in 1982 (*see* statement of earnings on page 10 of the report).

Example—

		Percent
1982 Operating Profit	$14,814,354	100.0
1983 Operating Profit	11,779,910	79.5
Decline	3,034,444	20.5
1981 Operating Profit	15,013,994	100.0
1982 Operating Profit	14,814,354	98.7
Decline	$ 119,640	1.3

As a percentage of net sales, operating profit dropped from 4.6% in 1982 to 3.7% in 1983. The decline is partially attributed to the increase in advertising, promotion, selling and administrative expenses of $3.4 million in 1983.

Example—

1983 operating profit of $11,779,910 divided by net sales of $313,719,923 gives a percentage of 3.7%. 1982 operating profit of $14,814,354 divided by net sales of $320,386,783 gives a percentage of 4.6%.

INTEREST COSTS

Interest expense increased 4.2% in 1983 compared to an increase of 63.3% in 1982. These percentages are provided by management on page 18. The actual interest costs are in the statement of earnings on page 10.

The increase in interest costs reflects a substantial increase in long-term debt from $2.6 million in 1979 to $20.9 million in 1983 which is shown in the five-year summary of selected data on page 20 of the report. The change from 1981 to 1982 was less dramatic, only $2.0 million, but the trend has been toward increased borrowing. On page 18 of the report, the company claims that increased borrowing was required for capital additions, acquisition, and working capital. The company has expanded into new foreign countries and has opened 26 new wholesale outlet stores.

EARNINGS COVERING INTEREST. The number of times interest is earned is measured by dividing operating profits before interest and taxes by the annual interest expense. For 1983, you divide operating profit of $11,-779,910 by interest costs of $6,640,912 to find that interest was earned 1.77 times. In 1982, interest was earned 2.32 times ($14,814,354 divided by $6,375,807). There was a decline in operating profits before interest and taxes without a corresponding decrease in interest expense. The company cannot afford to have this ratio decline any further, since the creditors would seriously question the company's ability to meet its interest obligation.

FOREIGN EXCHANGE PROBLEMS

Unfavorable foreign exchange rates contributed to the overall decline in sales. The foreign operations make up approximately 17% of total company sales, *see* geographic information on page 16 of the report.

The chairman's message on page 1 claims that sales and earnings would have been higher by $21.5 million and $3.5 million respectively, if foreign exchange rates had remained the same as the previous year.

The summary of significant accounting policies on page 13 states that in fiscal 1982 the company adopted the provisions of Financial Accounting Standards Board Statement No. 52 entitled "Foreign Currency Transactions." Balance sheet accounts are translated at the rates of exchange in effect at the Balance Sheet date. The income statement is translated using the average exchange rates prevailing throughout the period. The effects of the translation are recorded in two places in the financial statements. For those countries that are considered hyper-inflationary the realized gains and losses are recorded in the other (net) category of the statement of income. With a hyper-inflationary economy, unusual fluctuations should be expected. For those economies not considered hyper-inflationary the foreign currency translation is recorded in the stockholders' equity section of the Balance Sheet. In this case, the fluctuations should be much less. The Balance Sheet on page 11 of the report shows an insignificant change in the foreign currency translation account from 1982 to 1983. As you have seen in the annual report, the products are available in over 100 countries or geographic regions and therefore the foreign exchange situation will always exist.

DEBT RATIO

To measure the riskiness of a business from the creditors' point of view, you may figure the debt ratio to total assets. This tells how much of the assets are financed by the creditors. It is calculated by dividing long- and short-term debt by total assets. Looking at the Balance Sheet on page 11 of the report, you will find the percentage of assets financed by long- and short-term debt to be 32.4% for 1983 as compared to 30.7% in 1982.

Example—

$$1983 \text{ ratio: } \frac{\$55,977,002}{\$172,987,298} = 32.4\%$$

$$1982 \text{ ratio: } \frac{\$53,721,760}{\$175,014,938} = 30.7\%$$

Approximately one-third of the company's assets are financed by debt, which is fairly high leverage along with accompanying high interest costs. In times of business stress the company would be more secure if there was less debt. Interest payments are a fixed and steady cost, whereas dividend payments may be reduced or deferred.

Cash will become important to both the company and its creditors in 1986 when the maturities on the debt will be $16.6 million (*see* Note #5 on page 14). The company has at its disposal unused lines of credit of $49.5 million and has entered into a $50 million revolving credit agreement of which there were no borrowings as of September 30, 1983. Apparently, the creditors have faith in the ability of the company to pay their interest and principal on a timely basis.

TOTAL LIABILITIES TO TOTAL ASSETS

Total liabilities to total assets is calculated by dividing all liabilities (excluding stockholders' equity) by total assets. Using the data of the Balance Sheet on page 11 of the report, we can calculate that total liabilities are 60.2% of total assets for 1983 and 61.6% for 1982.

Example—

$$\text{1983 ratio: } \frac{\$104,114,317}{\$172,987,298} = 60.2\%$$

$$\text{1982 ratio: } \frac{\$107,730,831}{\$175,014,938} = 61.6\%$$

TOTAL STOCKHOLDERS' EQUITY TO TOTAL ASSETS

Total stockholders' equity to total assets is calculated by dividing stockholders' equity by total assets. Using the data of Balance Sheet on page 11 of the report, we can calculate that total stockholders' equity is 39.8% of total assets for 1983 and 38.4% for 1982.

Example—

$$1983 \text{ ratio}: \frac{\$68,872,981}{\$172,987,298} = 39.8\%$$

$$1982 \text{ ratio}: \frac{\$67,284,107}{\$175,014,938} = 38.4\%$$

PROVISIONS FOR INCOME TAX

On page 15 of the report, there is a breakdown of company tax liability. The effective 1983 tax rate of 22% was lower than the statutory tax rate of 46% primarily from adjustments of prior years' taxes, investment tax credits and foreign income taxed at lower rates.

The company follows the flow-through method for investment tax credits, taking the credit in the year it arises (*see* Note #1 to the financial statement on page 13 of the report). The source of the investment tax credits can be checked by reviewing the change in the property, plant, and equipment accounts in the Balance Sheet and the capital expenditures in the consolidated Statements of Changes in Financial Position on page 12 of the report. The company has made capital expenditures of $4.2 million, $9.0 million and $8.9 million in 1983, 1982 and 1981, respectively. A 10% investment tax credit would create a savings of $.4 million, $.9

million and $.9 million in 1983, 1982 and 1981, respectively.

Included in the provision for income taxes are deferred taxes reflecting timing differences in the recognition of revenue and expense for tax and financial statement purposes. The significant increase from 1982 to 1983 is partly due to a steady rise in depreciation. Another major increase is related to an election to treat promotional expenses as a direct deduction in the year they are incurred for tax purposes rather than amortize the expenses over more than a year for accounting purposes.

The company did not explain why foreign income was taxed at lower rates. The change from 1982 to 1983 in the foreign rates (Note #9 on page 15 of the report) can be determined by dividing the foreign income tax provisions (current and deferred) by the foreign earnings. For 1983, the rate is 39.8% and for 1982 the rate is 48.2%.

Example—

$$1983 \text{ rate: } \frac{\$1,313,000}{\$3,300,000} = 39.8\%$$

$$1982 \text{ rate: } \frac{\$2,023,000}{\$4,200,000} = 48.2\%$$

If the future foreign tax rates remain lower and the company can increase its foreign earnings, a favorable earnings situation may develop. International operations earnings of $13.1 million remain undistributed.

The company intends to permanently invest these earnings in future growth and expansion. Since the earnings have not been distributed to the U.S., no U.S. income taxes have been provided. But if they were distributed, the foreign income tax credits would substantially offset the U.S. income taxes.

CONSOLIDATED STATEMENT OF RETAINED EARNINGS

Even though net earnings were at their lowest point in three years, the company increased the dividend payment to its stockholders. In 1983, the company paid out over half of current earnings in dividends. The amounts available for dividends are reflected in the earnings per share data that are calculated by dividing net earnings by the weighted average shares of common stock outstanding (*see* Note #1 of the financial statements on page 13 of the report). The earnings per share were $1.01, $1.73, and $1.56 for 1983, 1982, and 1981, respectively.

Example—

$$1983 \text{ EPS: } \frac{\$3,908,612}{3,859,892 \text{ shares}} = \$1.01$$

The 1983 closing retained earnings balance represents approximately 41.2% of the total assets.

Example—

> Retained earnings of $71,346,773 divided by total assets of $172,987,298 gives the percentage 41.2%.

Restrictions have been placed on the use of these earnings by the lending institutions. In Note #5 on page 14 of the report the company states that $33.1 million of the retained earnings may be used to pay dividends and buy treasury stock. This leaves approximately $38.2 million as restricted. The amount of the restriction is understandable because of the amount of company debt.

RETURN ON INVESTMENT

The return on investment is an important measure to a stockholder. To make the calculation, you divide dividends paid per share by average price per share. The market prices of the stock and dividends per share for each quarter are shown in the report on page 19.

Example—

> Assume you purchased stock at $20 per share and received $.54 dividends per share, your return is 2.7% ($.54/$20). If you purchased stock at $10 per share, your return is 5.4% ($.54/$10). These are not satisfactory returns considering the current high savings bank rate.
> A stock showing a current return of 4 to 5% can-

not be attractive to investors unless there is an expectation of capital appreciation in the near future.

BOOK VALUE

As an investor, you may want to compare book value per share of common stock to the market price of the stock. To calculate this, you divide the total stockholders' equity from the Balance Sheet on page 11 or the selected financial data on page 20 of the report by the weighted average common shares outstanding in Note #1 of the financial statement on page 13 of the report. As of the closing Balance Sheet date, the book value per share for 1983 is $17.84, $17.68 for 1982, and $16.79 for 1981. These moderate increases in book value are attributable to retention of earnings.

Example—

$$\text{1983 book value:} \quad \frac{\$68,872,981}{3,859,892 \text{ shares}} = \$17.84$$

$$\text{1982 book value:} \quad \frac{\$67,284,107}{3,804,449 \text{ shares}} = \$17.68$$

$$\text{1981 book value:} \quad \frac{\$64,699,685}{3,854,405 \text{ shares}} = \$16.79$$

PRICE-TO-EARNINGS RATIO

To calculate price-to-earnings ratio, divide the market price per share shown on page 19 of the report by the earnings per share for the year on page 10 of the report. Using the data for the fourth quarter of 1983, the price-to-earnings ratio is 17.1 and 13.5, using high and low market prices per share during the quarter. For the fourth quarter for 1982 the ratios were 8.3 and 6.2, respectively.

Example—

$$\text{PE ratio 1983 high (4th quarter)}: \frac{\$17.25}{\$1.01} = 17.1$$

$$\text{PE ratio 1982 low (4th quarter)}: \frac{\$13.625}{\$1.01} = 13.5$$

$$\text{PE ratio 1982 high (4th quarter)}: \frac{\$14.375}{\$1.73} = 8.3$$

$$\text{PE ratio 1982 low (4th quarter)}: \frac{\$10.75}{\$1.73} = 6.2$$

Lower 1983 earnings directly contributed to the doubling of the price-to-earnings ratio in 1983. The market price of the stock in the first quarter of 1983 surged following the excellent 1982 earnings record. However, as net earnings for the last three quarters dropped, the market price of the stock fell.

WORKING CAPITAL

Since 1981, the company has been steadily increasing its working capital showing an increase of $13.1 million or 34.7%. The major source of the increase is the rise in long-term and short-term borrowings.

CURRENT RATIO. The current ratio calculated by dividing current assets by current liabilities is 1.64 to 1.00 for 1983 and 1.52 to 1.00 for 1982. This ratio is below the accepted standard of a 2 to 1 ratio, but it is not cause for alarm.

Example—

$$\text{1983 current ratio: } \frac{\$130,563,426}{\$79,737,790} = 1.64$$

$$\text{1982 current ratio: } \frac{\$131,806,996}{\$86,895,680} = 1.52$$

ACID RATIO TEST. A more stringent test of company ability to pay debts is the acid test ratio. It is calculated by subtracting inventories from current assets and dividing the total by all current liabilities. The acid ratio improved in 1983. It went from .78 to 1.0 in 1982 to .84 to 1.0 in 1983. A 1.0 to 1.0 ratio would be ideal, but the acid test and current ratio although slightly below the norm, is not critical in the case of an active concern such as the Alberto-Culver Company.

Example—

$$\text{1983 Acid Ratio: } \frac{\$66,766,438}{\$79,737,790} = .84$$

$$\text{1982 Acid Ratio: } \frac{\$67,488,648}{\$86,895,680} = .78$$

ACCOUNTS RECEIVABLE TURNOVER

The accounts receivable turnover is found by dividing the net sales for the year by the year-end accounts receivable balance (normally, you would use average receivables). The turnover for 1983 was 5.27 and 5.21 for 1982.

Example—

$$1983 \text{ turnover: } \frac{\$313,719,923}{\$59,533,065} = 5.27$$

$$1982 \text{ turnover: } \frac{\$320,386,783}{\$61,472,626} = 5.21$$

Further, by dividing 360 days by the turnover ratios for 1983 and 1982, you find that in both years it takes about 68 to 70 days to turn over the receivables. This seems higher than the norm, but the foreign credit terms are undoubtedly longer. There is a mix here, and the combined effect cannot be measured since credit terms are not mentioned in the report.

The Balance Sheet also shows that the bad debt allowance has declined from $1.8 million in 1982 to $1.6 million in 1983. Calculated as a percentage of gross receivables, the allowance was 2.54% and 2.77% for 1983 and 1982, respectively. This decline is favorable. Although the company has not supplied any data relevant to its credit policies or valuation methods, the economic recovery contributed to a degree to a lower accounts receivable and allowance for doubtful accounts.

RETURN ON TOTAL ASSETS

Using the selected financial data on page 20 of the report, you can calculate the return on total assets by dividing the net earnings by the average total assets for the year. The return on total assets for 1979 through 1983 was 4.0%, 10.0%, 4.6%, 4.1%, and 2.2%. This trend is favorable, except for the reversal in 1983 because of a 40.8% decline in net earnings.

Example—

$$1983 \text{ return}: \frac{\$3,908,612}{(\$172,987,298 + \$175,014,938) \div 2} = 2.2\%$$

RETURN ON STOCKHOLDERS' EQUITY

Using the selected financial data on page 20 of the report, you can calculate the return on stockholders' equity by dividing the net earnings by the average total stockholders' equity for the year. For the years 1979 through 1983, the return was 7.1%, 18.8%, 9.6%, 10.0% and 5.7%. The same trend was true with the return on total assets.

Example—

$$1983 \text{ return}: \frac{\$3,908,612}{(\$68,872,981 + \$67,284,107) \div 2} = 5.7\%$$

119

STOCK OPTIONS, TREASURY STOCK, PAID-IN CAPITAL

A stock option represents a right to buy a certain number of shares of stock at a specified price within a certain period of time. They are usually given to employees as part of a benefits or bonus program. The options have a specified life span and if not exercised, they are lost. The schedule in Note #6 of the report on page 14 shows the number of shares under option and the exercise prices. If someone were to exercise any of the options, they would realize a gain or loss for the difference in the exercise price and the fair market value of the stock. The stock is purchased from the company's own Treasury stock, not in the open marketplace. The difference in the exercise price and what the company originally paid for reacquiring its Treasury stock is booked to the Paid-In Capital account. Most of the options remaining were issued in 1983 at an exercise price of $21.81, which is about $4.00 higher than the fourth quarter market price high of $17.25. If the market price does not increase beyond the exercise price within five years, no one will exercise them and the options will become worthless.

PENSION PLAN

In Note #1 of the financial statement on page 13 there is a brief description of the accounting policy for pension costs. Normal service costs are accrued and funded currently. Prior service costs are amortized and funded over thirty years.

There has been an increase in 1983 pension expense of 43% as compared to an increase of 8.9% in 1982. The 1983 increase can be attributed to the company expansion requiring more employees. This trend should continue through 1984, since the company has stated in several instances in the report that it will continue to expand during 1984. The assets of the plan earned an estimated 8% return. The company has eight pension plans that are noncontributory on the employee's behalf. No details are given regarding the plans or the number of employees participating.

LEASES

The lease commitment schedule, in Note #10 of the annual report indicates the future fixed costs of capital-operating leases. Although rental expense for operating leases has risen from $4.9 million in 1981 to $7.5 million in 1983, there could be a substantial decline to follow in later years. The costs for operating leases are declining from a $4.8 million commitment in 1984 to $1.5 million in 1989 and later. Apparently several leases are expiring and if not renewed, the rental expenses will decline considerably. Capital leases are only a small portion of all leases. The commitment schedule indicates that no payments are required after 1987, at which point the company will own whichever properties they were leasing.

CASH AND SHORT-TERM INVESTMENTS

The short-term investments are carried at cost.

There has been an insignificant change of 7% from 1982 to 1983, and no specific notes are mentioned by the company.

CONSOLIDATED STATEMENT OF CHANGES IN FINANCIAL POSITION

The working capital format presented on page 12 of the report is similar to the one discussed in Chapter 4. As mentioned earlier, the working capital has increased steadily by $13.1 million since 1981.

The changes in long-term debt had a significant effect on the sources and uses of working capital. The increase of $13.0 million in 1982 appears to have been primarily used for capital expenditures of $9.0 million, while in 1983, the $15.1 million in borrowings was needed to pay off current maturities of $13.1 million. Note #5 of the annual report shows that the revolving credit note of $10 million was paid off in 1983, and a new 11% $15 million note was secured. This note is not due until 1985; therefore less working capital will be applied in 1984 toward the reduction of debt. More cash will probably be available in 1984 toward capital expenditures and increased dividends. In 1985, the company will probably refinance the $15 million note and the working capital effect will be negligible.

The other major sources of working capital are those items that have been deducted from net earnings, but do not involve an actual cash outlay, specifically depreciation, amortization, deferred income taxes and gains on sales of property, plant and equipment. They are simple accounting paper adjustments. They are added back to net earnings where they have been deducted from, so as to show the true sources of working capital provided by operations.

Depreciation has been steadily contributing to the increase in working capital.

Amortization of Goodwill and other intangible assets (trademarks) will continue to be a steady source of working capital, since they are amortized over extended periods of time. For goodwill, the period is 40 years and the amortization is the same each year. 1983 expenditures for trade names and goodwill amounted to $666,-812, an increase of $163,330 over 1982. These investments are a sign that a company is investing in future product expansion.

TREASURY STOCK. Treasury stock and stock options have little effect on the changes in working capital for 1983. We can relate this to the market price per share data on page 19 of the annual report. The lowest market price for the stock in 1982 was 10½ and the highest in 1983

123

was 24⅛. During 1982, $900,000 of treasury stock was issued to employee benefit plans, and in 1983 no treasury stock was issued. To maintain the current level of treasury stock, the company purchased $631,000 for treasury in 1982 and $473,000 in 1981. 1982 and 1981 market prices were much lower than in 1983. If 1984 market prices drop to the 1983 low market prices, the company will probably purchase more stock for treasury.

CASH DIVIDENDS continue to be a charge against working capital. Changes in stock options and treasury stock affect the amount of dividends paid. If all stock options were exercised, the company would have to pay dividends on an additional 55,074 shares. The more treasury stock that is purchased by the company, the less dividends it has to pay, unless the treasury stock is reissued to employees under the benefits program.

QUARTERLY FINANCIAL DATA

Note #12 of the annual report on page 17 displays comparative quarterly financial data for fiscal years 1982 and 1983. 1983 was more erratic compared to 1982. If it were not for the last quarter surge in 1983, the company's net earnings would have reached its lowest point in five years. The president attributed this rebound to the economic recovery.

ACCOUNTANT'S REPORT

The annual report is a nonqualified report with one exception. A nonqualified report simply means that the auditors agree with the financial information presented and have made substantial tests of the accounting records to support the company claim.

The exception mentioned pertains to consistency of accounting principles applied from period to period. The company changed its method of accounting for foreign currency translation in fiscal year 1982, which is not consistent with the method used in fiscal year 1981. If the change had a dramatic impact on the Balance Sheet, the amount would have been footnoted and highlighted in the accountant's report. But since the change was made in accordance with financial Accounting Standards Board Statement No. 52 and is a generally accepted accounting principle, the auditors concurred with this change.

SUMMARY

We hope that this analysis has shown you the technique of reviewing an annual report and the necessity of developing a picture from various sources scattered throughout the report. From the analysis, we have learned that the company is highly leveraged but has not experienced any problems in meeting its interest payments. The creditors are protected in case of a decline in earnings, by placing heavy restrictions on the company's retained earnings. With these borrowed funds, the company has been aggressive in new product development and expansion. Sales declines were attributable to two major uncontrollable events—foreign exchange rates and the economic recession. The company, however, weathered the crisis and its ability to keep sales at high levels and to show profits is a positive sign of its business strength. However, from the stockholder's viewpoint, dividend returns have been small. Any capital return will depend on the company increasing its sales and current return and winning investor confidence.